PRIMARY READING AND WRITING ACTIVITIES

for every month of the school year

PRIMARY READING AND WRITING ACTIVITIES for every month of the school year

Leslie Anne Perry, Ph.D.
Illustrated by **Carrie Oesmann**

THE CENTER FOR APPLIED
RESEARCH IN EDUCATION
West Nyack, New York 10995

10 9 8 7 6 5 4 3 2 1

Library of Congress Cataloging in Publication Data

Perry, Leslie Anne.
Primary reading and writing activities for every month of the school year / Leslie Anne Perry ; illustrated by Carrie Oesmann.
p. cm.
ISBN 0-87628-630-9
1. Reading (Primary)—Handbooks, manuals, etc. 2. Language arts (Primary)—Handbooks, manuals, etc. 3. Teaching—Aids and devices—Handbooks, manuals, etc. 4. Activity programs in education—Handbooks, manuals, etc. I. Center for Applied Research in Education. II. Title.
LB1525.4.P47 1990
372.4—dc20 90-31494
CIP

ISBN 0-87628-630-9

THE CENTER FOR APPLIED RESEARCH IN EDUCATION
BUSINESS & PROFESSIONAL DIVISION
A division of Simon & Schuster
West Nyack, New York 10995

Printed in the United States of America

About the Author

Leslie Anne Perry, Ph.D. has had a wide range of experience in reading education. She has served as a classroom teacher and remedial reading specialist at the elementary and middle-grade levels and has taught undergraduate and graduate reading education courses.

Dr. Perry is the coauthor of *Teaching the Reading Teachers* (Charles C. Thomas, 1983), *Teaching Basic Skills in Reading* (Charles C. Thomas, 1985), and *Fry's Instant Word Puzzles and Activities* (Prentice-Hall, 1987). Her articles about teaching reading have appeared in *Alabama Reader, Georgia Journal of Reading, Idaho Reading Report, Illinois Reading Council Journal, Indiana Reading Quarterly, Kentucky Reading Journal,* the *Michigan Reading Journal,* the *Mississippi Reading Journal,* the *Mississippi Educator, Ohio Reading Teacher,* the *Oklahoma Reader, Reading Improvement, Reading in Virginia,* the *Reading Instruction Journal,* the *Reading Teacher,* the *Tennessee Reading Teacher,* and the *Wisconsin State Reading Association Journal.*

Currently, Dr. Perry is an adjunct assistant professor at Appalachian State University in Boone, North Carolina. Her professional responsibilities include teaching "Language Arts in the Elementary School" and "Principles of Reading Instruction for the Classroom Teacher."

About This Resource

The purpose of *Primary Reading and Writing Activities for Every Month of the School Year* is to give you a wide variety of ready-to-use activities that allow your students to practice the reading and writing skills you have been teaching them. Many of the activity pages in this book encourage students to interact with the material—and they encourage students to *think.*

As an experienced teacher, I recognize the need to keep some groups of children engaged in learning activities while you are working directly with another group of children. However, I can also identify with the frustration teachers sometimes feel when they use materials whose primary purpose seems to be to keep children occupied. The reproducible pages in this book are not intended to be merely *busywork.*

For each month from September through May, you'll find the following topical, single-page, reproducible sheets:

- *Mini Poster*—featuring children reading or writing with pleasure
- *Cover for Language Experience Story*—with a title and appropriate art
- *Rebus Story*—with questions that test comprehension
- *Handwriting Practice*—a decorated sheet to make practice special
- *Nonfiction*—a factual story with accompanying questions
- *Let's Write a Letter*—a decorated letter form
- *Biography*—a profile with accompanying questions
- *Calendar*—a blank calendar form decorated for the month
- *Words to Use in Your Writing*—topical words for student writing
- *Book Cover for Creative Writing* and *Blank Pages for Book*—provide decorated materials for creating individual or class mini books
- *Book Report*—a decorated form suitable for all kinds of books
- *Fiction*—a short story with accompanying questions
- *Play*—a play in which the whole class can participate
- *My Journal*—a decorated journal page
- *My Poem*—a decorated page for writing poetry
- *Puzzle Page*—a word search for words that go with the month
- *Just for Fun*—a variety of puzzle sheets
- *Story Starter*—introduces a situation and has students complete it
- *Following Directions*—instructions for an activity you may want to do with your class, along with questions to test comprehension
- *Thinking/Writing Page*—open-ended questions to promote creative thinking
- *Fantasy*—a story followed by questions
- *Reading Award*—a blank, decorated form

At the end of the book you'll also find a form for students to record their independent reading through the year, and a complete answer key. A guide to using the various sheets and suggestions for related activities are included in "How to Use This Book."

I hope you and your students will enjoy using these materials as much as I enjoyed creating them. If you have any comments or suggestions, I'd appreciate hearing from you.

Leslie Anne Perry

Contents

How to Use This Book

Mini Poster

The division page for each month of the school year is designed to be used as a mini poster. You can copy it and use it *as is.* You can also copy it on white paper and color in portions of the picture, or copy it on colored paper. The mini poster can then be mounted on heavy paper and/or laminated.

These posters are also suitable for enlargement. You can place the page on an opaque projector and enlarge the picture for use on a bulletin board or as a door decoration. If an opaque projector is not available, a transparency can be made from the mini poster. The transparency can then be placed on an overhead projector and enlarged in that manner.

You will notice that the mini posters all show children involved in reading and/or writing activities. The posters, therefore, promote reading and writing as worthwhile pursuits.

Cover for Language Experience Story

Included in the activities for each month is a page to be used as a cover for language experience stories. While language experience stories are generally associated with kindergarten and first grade, older students also enjoy dictating stories that their teacher records either in writing or by using a tape recorder. (When older students are not slowed down by having to write the story themselves, they often create some extremely imaginative stories.)

After stories have been recorded on the chalkboard, chart tablet, or with a tape recorder, they can be typed or neatly written on 8½″ × 11″ paper. Books can then be made using the provided cover. These books can be produced for individual students, small groups of students, or an entire class.

For greater durability, the book cover can be mounted on poster board and laminated before attaching it to the story pages. A back cover can be made in a similar manner. These heavy-duty books can then be placed in the classroom or school library to provide reading pleasure for the remainder of the school year.

Rebus Story

The first reading selection each month, a rebus story, is about two girls named Leslie and Connie. The girls, who are sisters, engage in a variety of activities, each relating to the month in which the story occurs.

The rebus stories are followed by two comprehension questions which require written responses. The questions involve literal comprehension—recalling details.

Handwriting Practice

The handwriting practice pages are designed to make handwriting time a little more special. These pages can be used for either manuscript or cursive handwriting depending on the age of your students.

You may wish to keep these pages in a file after your students complete them. At the end of the school year, you can return them to your students so that they can each see how their writing has improved during the year.

Nonfiction

Included in each month's pages is a nonfiction selection related to that month. The selection contains factual information about the holidays and activities or characteristics usually associated with the month or with the season in which the month occurs.

Each nonfiction selection is followed by two comprehension questions for which the students will write their answers. These questions involve creative comprehension, where the students are to respond emotionally in some manner.

Let's Write a Letter

The reproducible pages called "Let's Write a Letter" can be used each month by your students to write a letter to whomever they wish. The format of these pages is open to accommodate a wide variety of letter writing activities. Your students may want to write to a pen pal, friend, or relative in another city. They can also write to one of their classmates or to a student in another classroom in their own school.

To promote writing (and reading!), some teachers initiate *letter exchanges*, where their students write and exchange letters with students in another classroom. Whether students exchange letters within their own classroom, or with students in other classrooms, a rural-type mailbox can be used to make the activity even more appealing.

Biography

Each month features a biography of a person who worked very hard to achieve his or her chosen goals or who devoted his or her life to helping other people. Included are a civil rights leader, an explorer, an Indian guide, a labor leader, Nobel Prize winners, Olympic gold medal winners, and presidents. Because these persons' lives represent worthwhile values, the biography selections can be used to supplement an ongoing character education program.

Following each biography selection are two comprehension questions that require written responses. The questions are on the creative level. Students become involved with the reading material by responding emotionally.

Calendar

Every month, your students can each have their own calendar. For younger students, filling in a calendar can provide practice in learning number sequence and in learning to recognize the names of the days of the week. For all students, the calendar can be a place to record holidays and special events that involve the entire class.

Third grade teachers can have their students write small numerals in the corner of each square in order to leave space to record when various assignments are due (for example, "book report due" or "group project on mountains due"). Recording dates of long-term projects helps students learn to budget their time—a skill they will need throughout their school years.

Words to Use in Your Writing

Students can use the words on these pages for a variety of writing activities throughout each month. The words can also be used as spelling words or included in handwriting lessons. You can have older students put the words in alphabetical order.

For younger students who do not yet know these words, you can write the words on cards and teach them as sight words before the students use them in their writing. Games can also be played to make learning the words an enjoyable activity.

These words can also be incorporated into student-made bulletin boards. Various students can draw pictures that illustrate selected words, and the words, along with their pictures, can be displayed.

Book Cover for Creative Writing/Blank Pages for Book

These reproducible pages are designed to be cut in half. The book cover page forms both a front and back cover for student-made books. The blank pages can be duplicated in sufficient quantities to satisfy even the most prolific writers in your classroom.

While "publishing" your own book is always special, these books can be made even more special in a variety of ways. You can reproduce the pages on colored paper and/or let your students decorate the covers as they wish. You can have a parent volunteer, teaching assistant, or other paraprofessional type each student's book pages to make it look more like a real book. (If you have access to a personal computer with a word processing program, your students can type their own books.) Before stapling, the covers can be glued to poster board and/or laminated.

For younger students, whose written or dictated story may be only a single typed page, class books can be compiled. A heavy-duty stapler or some other binding method can be used to fasten the classroom collection of stories into one book.

Duplicate copies of group books or individual books can be placed in the classroom, school, or community library. (When I used to put my students' books in our school library, the librarian reported that they were the only books some students wanted to read!)

Book Report

Students can use these pages to report on books they have read and enjoyed. You will notice that the forms are open-ended (the traditional categories included in book reports—setting, main characters, plot—have been omitted). This was done to encourage students to read and report on a variety of types of books, nonfiction as well as fiction. Since students are not restricted to reading a particular type of book just because it fits the book report form, they can select books in which they have a genuine interest.

You may wish to make completed book reports available to all your students. Learning what some students thought of a particular book can help other students decide whether or not they want to read it.

Occasionally, students will select books that they later find they simply do not like. Therefore, you might want to consider a system for book reports that allows credit for partially completed books. Such a system permits students to stop reading books they find boring or unappealing. They can record the number of pages read and then write what it was about the book that made them decide not to finish it. (Being forced to finish reading books they dislike can cause students to dislike reading altogether.)

Fiction

Among the reading selections included each month is a fiction selection. These stories are about Emily and Ryan, who are next-door neighbors. Emily and Ryan are the children featured each month on the division page/mini poster, and the fiction selections are related to the activities depicted on those pages. These, as you may recall, all involve reading and/or writing in some way.

The fiction selections are followed by two comprehension questions for which students will supply written responses. The questions involve inferential comprehension—predicting outcomes and drawing conclusions.

Play

Each month a play is included to allow your students to participate in an enjoyable reading activity that develops social skills as well as language arts skills. The plays include parts for boys and girls in addition to the principal characters. This allows all your students to participate rather than just a select few.

After a little practice, most students enjoy putting on a play for an audience. However, *audience* does not have to mean parents and members of the community. Students from another classroom can be the audience.

To make the plays even more special, you can let different groups of students put on a play for the rest of your class, and you can videotape all the performances. Even though they are being taped, the students can read from their scripts. I have done this on a day just before my students were dismissed for a holiday. Putting on the plays and then watching them on television made a great learning activity on a day when my students were definitely activity oriented.

My Journal

The journal pages can be reproduced in as large a quantity as desired, depending on the needs of your students. For younger students using invented spelling, one page each month may be sufficient. Third grade students, however, could write a journal page for each school day of each month.

Encourage your students to write about whatever they want when they are writing journal pages. The primary purpose of these pages is to encourage writing. Your students' writing will develop and grow if they are allowed to record their thoughts in any manner they choose.

Your students may enjoy sharing their journal pages with other students. Various students may want to read their pages aloud to a small group or to the entire class.

My Poem

These pages give your students the opportunity to write poetry for their own enjoyment or to share with others. The pages are open-ended to allow for a wide variety of poetry-writing activities. Young students can write or dictate mini poems containing only a few words. Their poems may contain some rhyming words or no rhyming words, whatever you and your students prefer.

Older students may enjoy writing longer poems and poems that conform to a particular pattern, such as quatrain, cinquain, or haiku. Language arts books can be consulted for examples of these and other types of structured poems.

Puzzle Page

On these activity pages, your students search for hidden words and circle them. In each puzzle, the words all relate to the designated month. The words appear either horizontally (left to right only) or vertically (top to bottom only).

Just-for-Fun Page

On the just-for-fun pages, the format varies each month. On these pages, words are used that pertain to the month in which the activity appears. The pages are designed to provide appealing activities that enable students to learn and have fun at the same time. Directions for completing each type of activity are included.

Story Starter

Story starters are included each month to provide motivation for your students' story writing. These pages set the stage, and your students are then free to create stories that go in any direction they choose. These open-ended stories promote creativity as well as writing skills.

You may wish to have younger students dictate story endings while you write them. The stories can then be made into a class storybook.

These story starter pages make excellent material for oral reading activities. Your students can read aloud the stories they have created; and you can encourage expressive reading.

Following Directions

To provide students with practice in reading written directions, a following-directions page is included each month. These pages contain instructions for a variety of projects that can be completed in a primary classroom with teacher preparation and supervision. These projects include making play clay, making a jack-o-lantern, making pinecone turkeys, making holiday cookies, making mini snowflakes, making a Valentine box, making pinwheels, planting bean seeds, and making Mother's Day necklaces.

Each following-directions page has two comprehension questions relating to the information presented on the page. These questions involve literal comprehension (recalling sequence) and require students to write their responses.

Thinking/Writing Page

These pages, which go by various titles, all promote creative thinking on the part of the students. The activities allow students to use their imaginations.

The thinking/writing pages are open-ended—there are no right or wrong answers. Encourage students to be creative and follow their intuitions.

Fantasy

A different fantasy selection is included for every month of the school year. The characters in the fantasy selections are Tim and Mike. These boys are good friends who engage in a variety of activities. These make-believe stories include a talking animal, changing into someone else, going back in time, changing size, getting older and bigger, a giant Valentine, a little leprechaun, a magic rug, and making things magically happen.

After each fantasy selection is a comprehension question for which students will write out the answer. The question involves critical comprehension—distinguishing fantasy from reality.

Reading Award

The final page for each month is a reproducible reading award. As with other pages, these forms are open-ended. They allow you to write in the areas for which you want to use the awards. The awards can be presented to children for evidence of progress in any reading-related activity, from completing a level of your basal reading series, to learning a specific set of sight words, to exhibiting improved behavior during reading class.

Books I've Read This School Year

This form appears at the end of the May section, and can be used by your students throughout the school year to record the titles of books they have read. The forms can be kept in individual file folders so that students can independently record their titles. You may wish to have your students include their book reports in the folders, too.

Answer Keys

For many of the pages in this book, there are no right or wrong answers. For the pages where specific responses are required, answers are provided in the answer key section.

SEPTEMBER

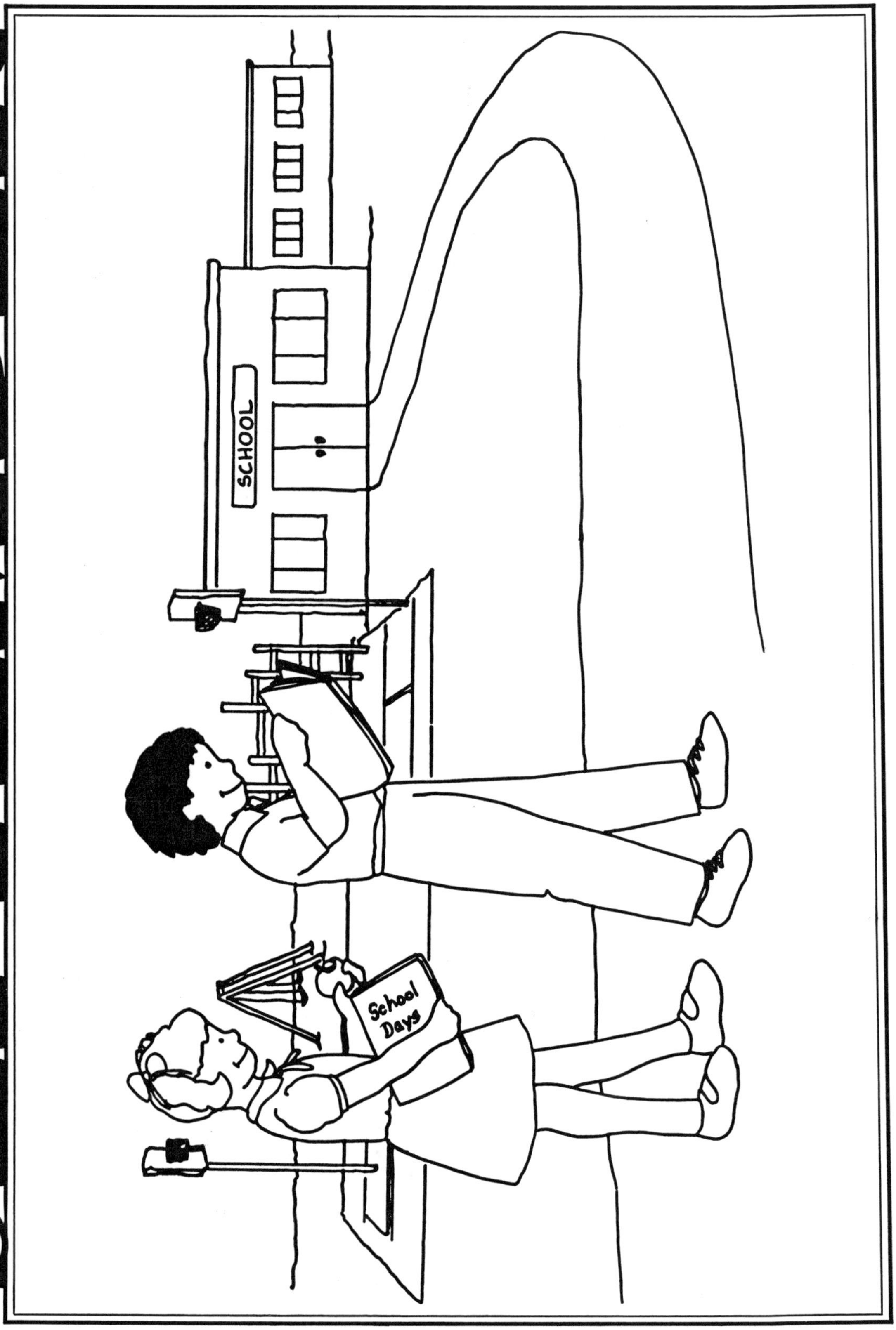

MY SUMMER FUN

Name ____________________

Rebus Story: Buying School Things

Soon it would be time for school to start.  Leslie and  Connie needed things for school. So they went to the 

.

"I need some  pencils," said  Leslie. "So do I," said  Connie. So both girls got  pencils.

"I need  paper," said  Connie. "I don't," said  Leslie. "I still have a lot from last year." So  Connie got some  paper, but  Leslie did not.

"Look," said  Leslie. "There is 

. I need 

." "Yes," said  Connie. "We'll both get 

."

"I think that is all we need," said  Connie. "We both have  scissors from last year. Are you ready to go?"

Questions: Literal Comprehension—Recalling Details

1. What things did  Leslie buy for school?

____

2. What things did  Connie buy for school?

____

Handwriting Practice

Name ____________________

Name ________________________

Nonfiction: September

September is *back-to-school* time for many boys and girls. Some children start back to school in August. But most people start the new school year after Labor Day. Labor Day is the first Monday in September.

Starting a new school year is usually a happy time. It is a time to see old friends. It is a time to make new friends.

When school first starts, some children miss sleeping late. They miss playing all day. But soon they get used to going to school. They have fun with their school friends. And they have fun learning new things. Then, if they are sick one day, they miss going to school!

Questions: Creative Comprehension—Responding Emotionally

1. What do you like most about going to school?

____

____

____

____

2. What do you like least about going to school?

____

____

____

____

Let's Write a Letter

Name ______________________________

Biography: Cesar Chávez

Cesar Chávez was born in 1927 in Arizona. His family had a small farm there. But they lost their farm during the Great Depression. They moved to California when Cesar was ten years old.

In California, Cesar's parents became migrant farm workers. They moved from place to place to pick the crops. When he was in the eighth grade, Cesar dropped out of school. He began working in the fields, too.

In 1962, Cesar Chávez started a union called the National Farm Workers Association. He wanted farm workers to be paid a fair amount for the work they did. The union helped to see that they were paid fairly.

In 1968, Chávez fasted (did not eat) for twenty-five days. He did this to support a grape strike. He wanted the people who grew grapes to pay a fair wage to the people who picked the grapes. He went without food so people would think about farm workers' problems.

Labor Day honors farm workers and all other workers in the United States. Each year, Labor Day is held the first Monday of September.

Questions: Creative Comprehension—Responding Emotionally

1. Cesar Chávez worked hard to help farm workers. Do you think it is important to work hard at what you do? Why or why not?

____

____

2. When you work hard and do a good job in school, how do you feel? On the back of your paper, write about how you feel when you do your work well.

Name ______________________

SEPTEMBER

Sunday	Monday	Tuesday	Wednesday	Thursday	Friday	Saturday

Name ______________________________

Words to Use in Your Writing

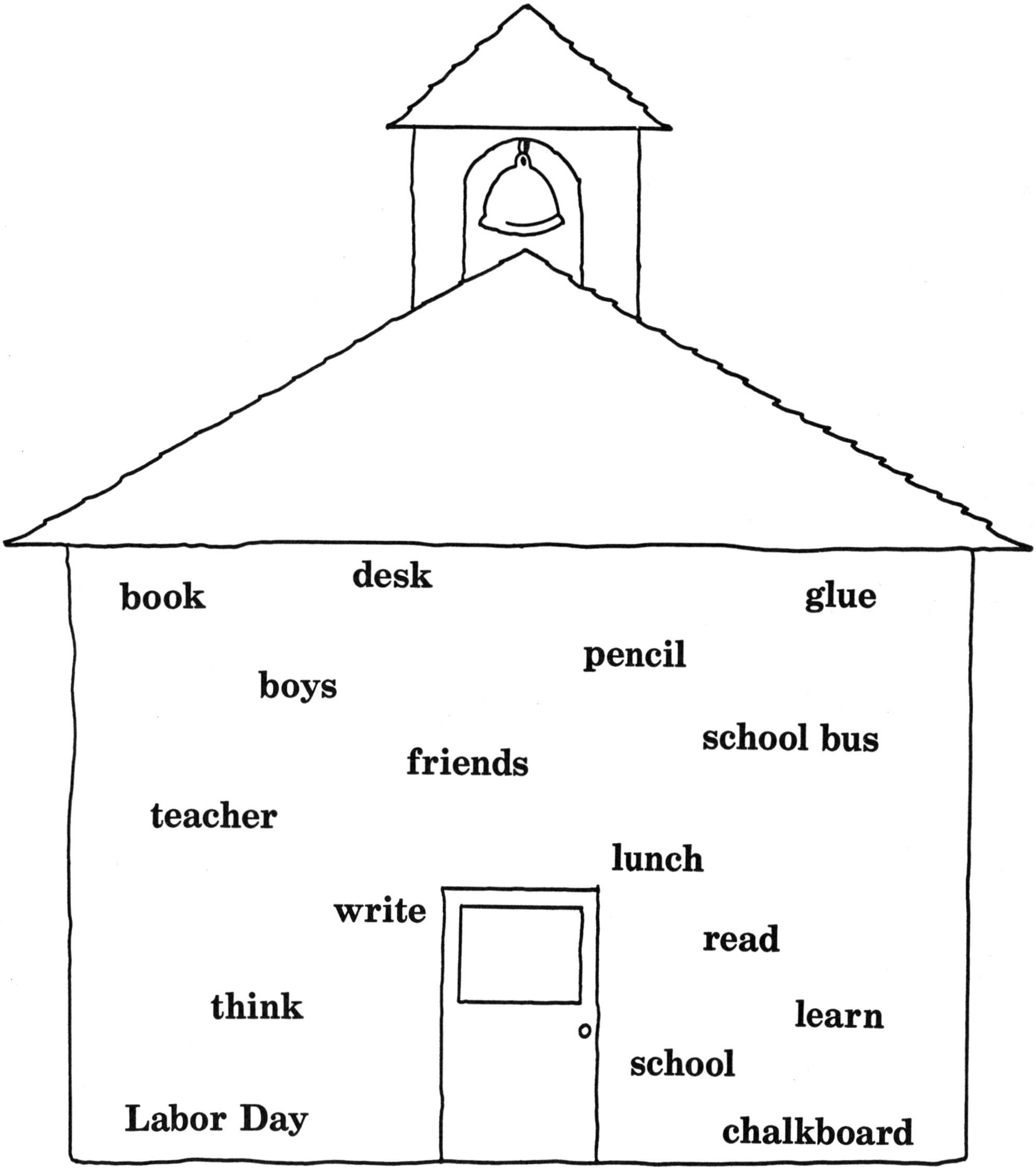

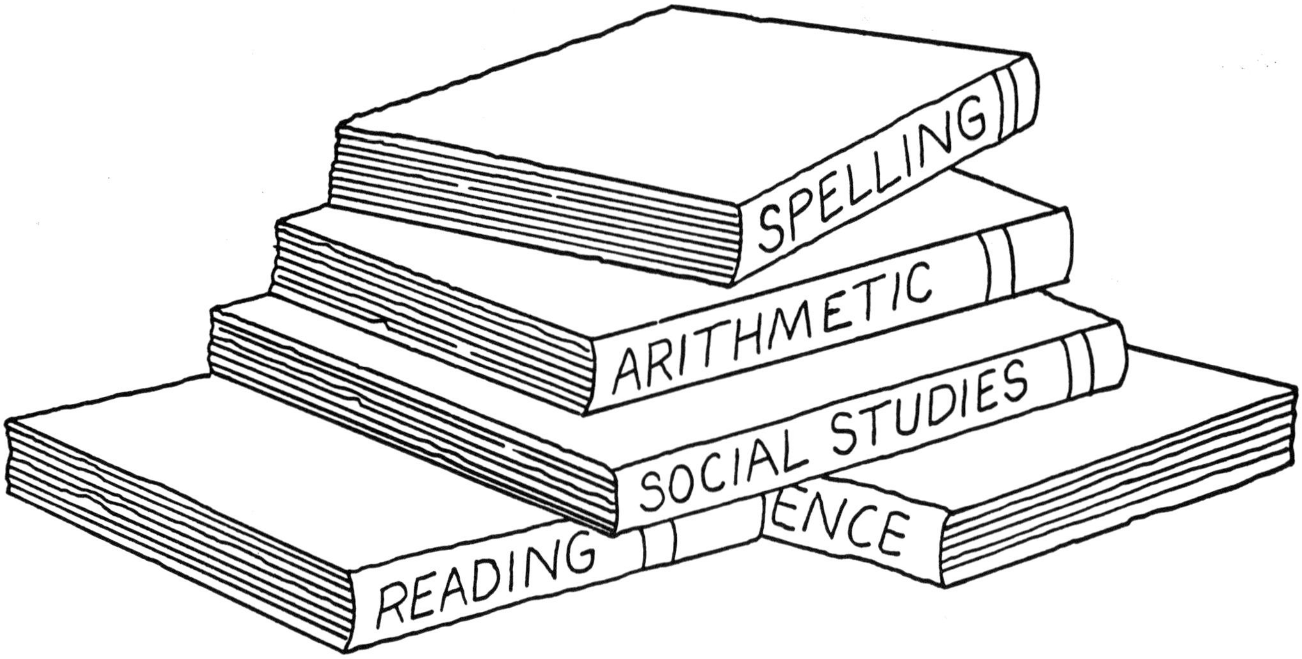

SEPTEMBER

SCHOOL BUS

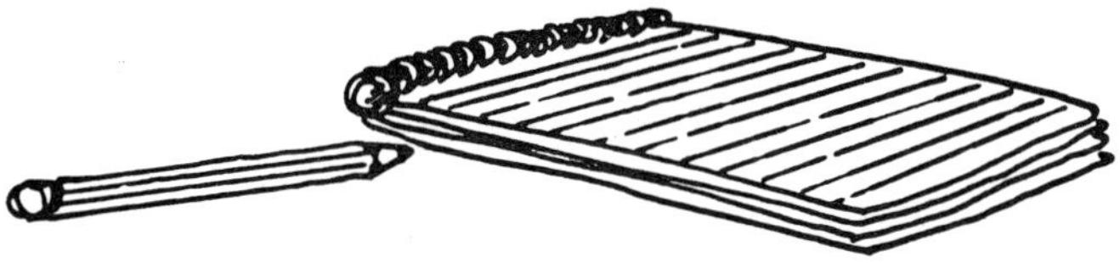

Name ____________________

Book Report

Title: ____________________

Author: ____________________

What the Book Was About:

____

____

____

____

____

____

____

My Reaction to the Book:

____

____

____

____

____

____

Name ____________________

Fiction:
The First Day of School

It was the first day of the new school year. Emily and Ryan were walking to school. Their school was near where they lived.

Emily and Ryan both moved in the summer. Now they live next door to each other. And they are both going to a new school.

"I wonder if I'll have any friends at this school," said Emily.

"I'm sure you will," said Ryan. "I wonder if I'll have a nice teacher."

Soon Emily and Ryan got to school. After they went in, they found out they were in the same class. Emily saw three people she knew. Ryan saw two people he knew.

Just then the new principal came in. "Your teacher is not here today," she said. "I will be with you until another teacher can get here."

Questions: Inferential Comprehension—
Predicting Outcomes and Drawing Conclusions

1. What do you think will happen next?

____

____

____

2. Do you think Emily and Ryan like their new school? Why or why not?

____

____

____

Name ________________________________

Play:
The Soccer Game

Characters:	Kyle	Beth	Prop: one soccer ball
	Roger	Carol	
	Trevor	Nancy	
	Boys	Girls	

Boys: *Today the Strikers are playing their big soccer game. Kyle, Roger, and Trevor are on their way to the game.*

Kyle: I really like to play soccer. I'm glad you talked me into going out for the team, Roger.

Roger: I'm glad you're on our team. You are a good player. We're going to need you today when we play the Rowdies!

Trevor: I would really like to beat the Rowdies! They beat us ten to zero the last time we played them!

Girls: *Beth, Carol, and Nancy get to the soccer field at the same time. They all play soccer for the Strikers.*

Beth: Hi everybody! Are we ready for the big game?

Carol: We sure are! I hope we can beat the Rowdies!

Nancy: I hope we beat them, too! The last time we played them, they blocked one of my best kicks. And one of their players knocked me down—on purpose!

(Kyle, Roger, Trevor, Beth, Carol, and Nancy are on the field. They line up and start playing soccer. They pass the soccer ball back and forth with their feet.)

Boys: *The game begins. The Strikers have the ball. They pass it back and forth. Down the field they go! They are almost to the goal!*

Carol: Kyle, I think I can score from here. Pass me the ball!

Kyle: O.K. Here it is!

(Kyle passes the ball to Carol. Carol scores a goal.)

Trevor: Hooray for Carol! She scored our first goal!

Girls: *In the first half of the game, the Strikers score two more goals. But the Rowdies score four goals. The Rowdies are winning by one goal.*

Roger: They are still winning. We need to score some more goals.

Nancy: If we try really hard this second half, maybe we can beat them.

Boys: *In the second half, the Strikers score three goals and the Rowdies score two goals. The score is tied six to six. There is only one minute left in the game. The Strikers have the ball.*

Beth: Kyle, can you get a kick from there?

Kyle: I think so! Pass me the ball!

(Beth passes the ball to Kyle. Kyle scores a goal.)

Roger, Trevor, Beth, Carol, Nancy: Hooray! Kyle scored a goal! We are ahead by one goal!

Girls: *The Rowdies start down the field toward their goal. Before they get there, the whistle blows. The game is over. The Strikers win the game by one goal!*

Kyle, Roger, Trevor, Beth, Carol, Nancy: Hooray! Hooray! We won! We won! We won!

Name ____________________

My Journal

Name ____________________

My Poem

____

Name ______________________

Puzzle Page: Word Search

Directions: Look for these words and circle them when you find them: book, boys, bus, chalkboard, desk, friends, girls, learn, lunch, pencil, read, school, teacher, think, write.

L	B	G	I	R	L	S	T	B	O	Y	S	W	D
D	R	E	O	D	B	V	W	M	R	C	I	S	A
P	F	X	K	F	R	I	E	N	D	S	Z	J	W
E	R	W	R	I	T	E	Q	S	I	Y	D	S	R
N	H	Z	I	O	V	H	T	Y	I	B	U	L	E
C	B	T	E	A	C	H	E	R	E	O	W	X	A
I	R	J	K	T	H	I	N	K	R	O	F	S	D
L	E	Q	Z	P	U	N	B	Y	D	K	D	X	L
E	S	T	L	E	A	R	N	R	U	G	F	O	B
R	C	X	P	U	T	G	K	D	E	S	K	R	U
I	H	F	C	V	M	O	P	E	F	I	T	Y	S
T	O	U	G	L	U	N	C	H	R	W	Q	V	M
D	O	R	V	I	D	X	M	Y	N	R	U	J	K
E	L	X	C	H	A	L	K	B	O	A	R	D	J

Name ______________________________

Just for Fun: Spell the Words

Directions: Cut apart the letters on this page. Then use the letters to spell each of these words: book, boys, bus, chalkboard, desk, friends, girls, learn, lunch, pencil, read, school, teacher, think, write.

a	b	c	d	e
f	g	h	i	k
l	n	o	p	r
s	t	u	w	y

Name ____________________

Story Starter: The Bus Ride

You are riding home on a school bus. You are busy talking to your friends. After a while, all your friends have gotten off the bus. You did not get off when the bus went by your house! What will you do? Write about it.

Name ____________________

Following Directions: How to Make Play Clay

You and your friends can make play clay. The first thing you will need is flour. Put four cups of flour into a bowl.

Next, you will need salt. Put one cup of salt in the bowl. Then mix the flour and salt together.

You can color your play clay if you want to. Choose a color you like. Put some dry tempera paint of that color in the bowl. Then mix it all up.

Now you are ready to add water. But only add a little water at a time. Work the water in well before you add more. You will know you have enough water when your play clay is soft and easy to work with. If you use too much water, your play clay will be sticky and hard to work with.

When your play clay is all mixed, you can make something with it. When you are not using your play clay, keep it in a bowl with a tight lid. You don't want your play clay to dry out!

Questions: Literal Comprehension—Recalling Sequence

1. What do you do after you put the flour in the bowl?

____

____

2. After you put in the paint and mix it, what do you do?

____

____

Name ______________________________

Thinking/Writing Page: Think about It

Think about a perfect school. What would it look like? What would it have in it? What would you do there? Write about what you think a perfect school would be like.

____

____

____

____

____

____

____

____

____

____

____

____

____

____

____

Name ____________________

Fantasy: The Talking Dog

Mike and Tim were walking to school. They walked past a big dog in its doghouse. "Hi, boys," said the dog.

"Hi, dog," said Tim and Mike. Then they walked on.

"Wait!" said Mike. "Dogs don't talk!"

"You're right," said Tim. "Let's go back."

The boys walked back to where the dog was. "You just talked," said Tim.

"That's right, I did," said the dog.

"But dogs don't talk," said Mike.

"I do," said the dog.

"What can you say?" asked Tim.

"I can say everything you can say," said the dog.

"Wait here," said Mike. "We want to go get some of our friends. We want them to see you, too."

So Mike and Tim went to get their friends. When they got back, the dog was gone.

Question: Critical Comprehension—Distinguishing Fantasy from Reality

1. What happened in this story that could not really happen?

____

____

____

____

____

READING AWARD

_______________ Is Presented

With This Award For:

____

____

____

Signed _______________

Date _______________

OCTOBER

WHEN I GET BIG

Name ______________________________

Rebus Story: The Halloween Party

It would soon be Halloween. 

and 

were going to have a party. 

called all their friends on the 

.

started getting together some good things to eat. They would have 

and 

and 

. 

got out a 

. She cut the 

and made a 

. Then she put the 

on the table next to where the food would go.

The next day, all their friends came to the party. They played games and ate 

, 

, and 

. Everyone had a great time!

Questions: Literal Comprehension—Recalling Details

1. What did they eat at the party?

____

2. What did 

make for the party?

____

Handwriting Practice

Name ________________________________

Name ____________________

Nonfiction: October

In many places, fall begins in October. The nights start getting colder. The leaves on the trees turn many pretty colors. Some children like to build leaf houses and play in the pretty leaves.

In October, it is sometimes cold in the mornings, too. Children start wearing jackets to school. Then, sometimes, it gets warmer during the day. When it does, they carry their jackets home instead of wearing them!

Halloween comes in October. It is on October 31. At many schools, there are Halloween parties. Children dress in costumes and get treats from their teachers.

October is a month of changes. It is a month for having fun, too.

Questions: Creative Comprehension—Responding Emotionally

1. What do you like most about the month of October?

____

____

____

2. Write about some of the things you like to do in October. Use the back of your paper if you need to.

____

____

____

Let's Write a Letter

Name ______________________________

Biography: Christopher Columbus

Columbus Day is the second Monday in October. Columbus Day honors Christopher Columbus.

Christopher Columbus was born in Italy in 1451. In 1492, he and his crew bravely sailed from Spain on three ships. The ships were called the Niña, the Pinta, and the Santa Maria.

When Columbus left Spain, he was looking for a new route to India, China, and Japan—which were called the Indies. The King and Queen of Spain paid for his trip. They wanted people in Spain to have an easier way to get things like spices and gold.

On October 12, 1492, Columbus reached what he thought was the Indies. But instead of being near China and Japan, he was very near what is now America. So people say that Columbus discovered America, or found a New World.

Columbus made four trips to the New World. After his last trip, he went back to Spain. He died on May 20, 1506, at the age of fifty-four.

Questions: Creative Comprehension—Responding Emotionally

1. If you had lived in Columbus's time, would you like to have sailed with him to the New World? Why or why not?

____

____

2. What do you think it would have been like to go on one of Columbus's ships and discover America? On the back of your paper, write about what it would have been like.

Name ____________________

OCTOBER

Sunday	Monday	Tuesday	Wednesday	Thursday	Friday	Saturday

Name ____________________

Words to Use in Your Writing

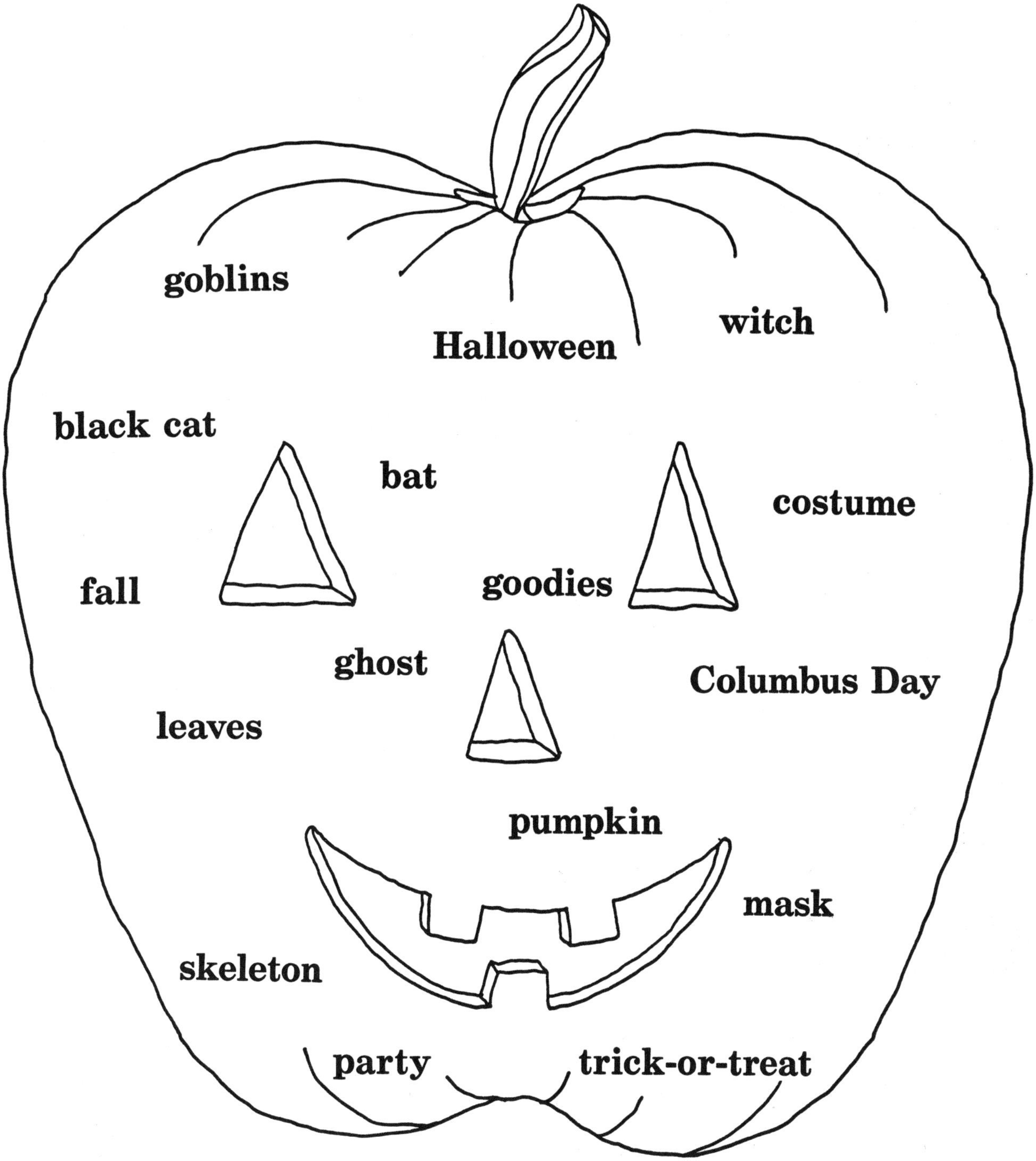

OCTOBER

Name ______________________

Book Report

Title: ______________________

Author: ______________________

What the Book Was About:

____

____

____

____

____

____

____

My Reaction to the Book:

____

____

____

____

____

____

Name ______________________________

Fiction:
A Scary Afternoon

One afternoon, Emily and Ryan were sitting in a big chair. They were reading a good book. The book was about monsters.

As they read the book, they started to get a little scared. They knew there was no such thing as a monster. But reading about monsters was still kind of scary.

When they had read all but a few pages, they heard a loud crash in the kitchen. Then they heard a loud screech.

"What was that?" asked Emily.

"I don't know," said Ryan. "Let's go find out."

Emily and Ryan got up from the chair and walked slowly toward the kitchen. They were really getting scared. But they kept on walking. They wanted to know what made the crash and the screech.

When they got to the kitchen door, Ryan's black cat, Mickey, ran quickly past them. Then they looked into the kitchen and saw what made the crash. On the floor was the dish drainer and lots of pots and pans. Mickey had knocked them off the counter!

Questions: Inferential Comprehension—
Predicting Outcomes and Drawing Conclusions

1. What do you think Emily and Ryan will do next?

____

____

2. Do you think Emily and Ryan are still scared? Why or why not?

____

____

Name ______________________________

Play: Raking Leaves

Characters:	Ty	Anne	Props: one leaf rake
	Jay	Nancy	one football
	Todd	Julie	one long jump-rope
	Boys	Girls	one Frisbee®

Boys: *It is a cool fall afternoon. Ty is raking leaves in his family's yard. Jay comes over. He is carrying a football.*

Jay: Hi there! Would you like to throw my football with me?

Ty: No, I can't. My mother said I have to rake the leaves before I can play.

Jay: I'll help you. I'll go home and get my rake.

Girls: *So Jay goes home to get his rake. While he is gone, Anne and Nancy come over. They are carrying a long jump-rope.*

Anne: Hi there! Would you like to play jump rope with us?

Ty: No, I can't. My mother said I have to rake the leaves before I can play.

Nancy: We'll help you. We'll go home and get our rakes.

Boys: *So Anne and Nancy go home to get their rakes. While they are gone, Todd and Julie come over. They are carrying a Frisbee.*

Todd: Hi there! Would you like to throw a Frisbee with us?

Ty: No, I can't. My mother said I have to rake the leaves before I can play.

Julie: We'll help you. We'll go home and get our rakes.

Girls: *So Todd and Julie go home to get their rakes. Soon all Ty's friends come back. Jay has a football, but no rake. Anne and Nancy have a jump-rope, but no rakes. Todd and Julie have a Frisbee, but no rakes.*

Ty: Hi everybody! Where are your rakes?

Jay I couldn't bring our rake. My Dad was using it to rake the leaves in our yard.

Anne: I couldn't bring a rake, either. My brother was using our rake.

Nancy: My sister was raking the leaves in our yard. So I couldn't bring a rake, either.

Todd: I couldn't find our rake. I looked all over.

Julie: I found our rake. But my Mom said she was getting ready to use it to rake the leaves in our yard.

Ty: That's OK, everybody. While you were all gone to get your rakes, I finished raking all our leaves! Now I'm ready to throw a football with Jay, jump rope with Anne and Nancy, and throw a Frisbee with Todd and Julie! Let's play!

Name ________________

My Journal

____

Name ____________________

My Poem

____

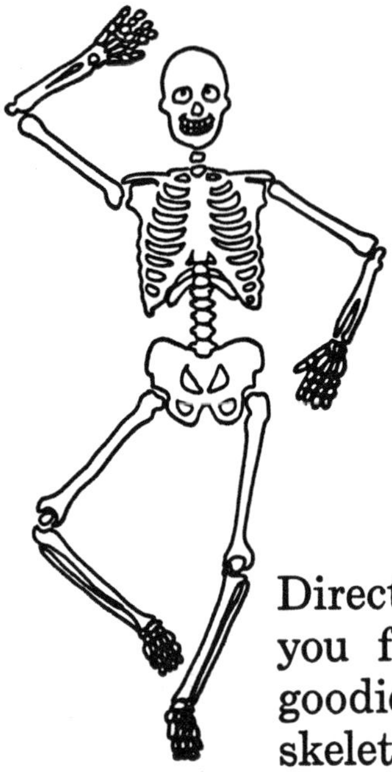

Name ______________________________

Puzzle Page: Word Find

Directions: Look for these words and circle them when you find them: bat, cat, costume, fall, ghost, goblins, goodies, Halloween, leaves, mask, party, pumpkin, skeleton, trick, treat, witch.

Y	H	A	L	L	O	W	E	E	N	I	P	E	R
F	D	C	V	P	B	M	W	T	R	E	A	T	W
P	G	G	H	O	S	T	E	X	M	K	U	J	W
A	E	Q	W	M	A	S	K	R	T	W	D	X	G
R	C	Q	X	O	P	C	M	V	R	E	S	Z	O
T	O	R	W	I	T	C	H	B	I	O	P	F	B
Y	S	G	F	J	K	I	R	M	C	I	U	S	L
K	T	I	L	E	A	V	E	S	K	I	M	X	I
D	U	R	T	B	A	T	O	D	Q	M	P	V	N
R	M	U	N	E	I	O	R	T	F	W	K	A	S
I	E	I	T	M	C	A	T	X	A	Z	I	Q	W
R	P	G	O	O	D	I	E	S	L	R	N	D	S
Y	X	O	G	K	L	J	R	S	L	C	O	R	I
R	S	K	E	L	E	T	O	N	U	O	P	V	B

Name ______________________

Just for Fun: Word Scramble

Directions: Unscramble the Halloween words and write them in their correct form on each line. Look for these words: bat, black cat, costume, ghosts, goblins, goodies, Halloween, mask, party, pumpkin, skeletons, spooky, treats, tricks, witch.

atb	aksm	saertt
1. ____________	2. ____________	3. ____________
kpmupin	yoskpo	ssthgo
4. ____________	5. ____________	6. ____________
aklkc tca	skicrt	usocetm
7. ____________	8. ____________	9. ____________
dgieoso	bogsnli	yrpta
10. ____________	11. ____________	12. ____________
twchi	ktossleen	wlHleoena
13. ____________	14. ____________	15. ____________

Name ____________________

Story Starter: A Scary Night

You and a friend are in a graveyard late at night. The wind is blowing. It is very dark. Suddenly a hand reaches up from one of the graves. What happens next? Write about it.

Name ________________________________

Following Directions: How to Make a Jack-O-Lantern

For Halloween, many people make jack-o-lanterns. To make a jack-o-lantern, start with a pumpkin. It is a good idea to clean off the outside if there is any dirt on the pumpkin.

After the pumpkin is clean, cut out a round place on the top of the pumpkin. This part can be the jack-o-lantern's hat.

Next, clean out all the insides of the pumpkin. You can save the insides to make a pumpkin pie. You can also save the seeds and bake them. Baked pumpkin seeds are good to eat.

After the inside of the pumpkin is cleaned out, cut out places for the eyes, nose, and mouth. You can make your jack-o-lantern look either happy or sad by the way you make its mouth!

After you have finished cutting your jack-o-lantern, you are ready to put a light in it. You can use either a candle or a small flashlight. Then, when Halloween comes, you will have your very own jack-o-lantern!

Questions: Literal Comprehension—Recalling Sequence

1. What do you do after you clean the outside of the pumpkin?

____

____

2. After you clean out the inside of the pumpkin, what do you do next?

____

____

Name ______________________

Thinking/Writing Page: Using Your Head

Heads are places to put hats. But heads are mostly used for thinking and learning. You have learned a lot since you started going to school. Write about some of the most interesting things you have learned.

Name ____________________

Fantasy: Trying on Costumes

Tim and Mike were trying on costumes at the store. They both needed costumes to wear to the Halloween party.

Tim tried on an astronaut's costume. Right after he put it on, he started to feel funny. He closed his eyes. When he opened them, he was inside a spaceship. He could see the earth out of the window. He closed his eyes again. When he opened them, he was back in the costume store.

"Where have you been?" asked Mike. "I've been waiting for you for an hour. You were standing right here and then you were gone!"

"I'm not sure where I was," said Tim.

"I like this firefighter's costume," said Mike. "I think I'll try it on."

Right after Mike put on the firefighter's costume, he started to feel funny. He closed his eyes. When he opened them, he was riding in a big firetruck. The truck was racing to a fire. Mike could see flames shooting out of the windows of a tall building. He closed his eyes again. When he opened them, he was back in the costume store.

"Where have you been?" asked Tim. "I've been waiting for you for an hour. You were standing right here and then you were gone!"

"I'm not sure where I was," said Mike. "But it's time to go now."

"Don't you want to buy a costume?" asked Tim.

"No," said Mike. "I think I'll just wear a mask to the party."

Question: Critical Comprehension—Distinguishing Fantasy from Reality

1. Could this story really happen? Why or why not? Write your answer on the back of your paper.

READING AWARD

_______________________________ Is Presented

With This Award For:

____

____

____

Signed _______________________

Date _______________________

NOVEMBER

THINGS I AM THANKFUL FOR

Name ______________________________

Rebus Story: Choosing a Book

One Saturday morning,  Leslie and  Connie went to the  . It was Children's Book Week. There were many new  books in the  .

"Oh, look," said  Connie. "Here is a  book about a  horse. I'm going to check out this  book."

"I found a  book about a funny  rabbit," said  Leslie. "I'm going to check it out."

"I want to check out two  books," said  Connie. "I'm going to check out this one about  flags, too. Do you want this one on  flowers? I know you like  flowers."

"Yes," said  Leslie. "I do want that  book on  flowers. Let's sit over here and read for a while. Then we can check out our  books."

Questions: Literal Comprehension—Recalling Details

1. Which books is  Connie going to check out?

____

2. Which books is  Leslie going to check out?

____

Handwriting Practice

Name ______________________

Name ________________________________

Nonfiction: November

When people think of November, they often think of Thanksgiving. Thanksgiving is the fourth Thursday in November. It is a time when people give thanks for what they have.

The first Thanksgiving in America was held in 1621. It lasted three days. The Pilgrims gave thanks for the food they had. They also gave thanks because they had made it through the winter.

Besides Thanksgiving, there are other special days in November. Veterans Day is November 11. It is the day we honor men and women who are veterans. Veterans are people who have served in the Armed Forces—the Army, Navy, Air Force, or Marines.

Children's Book Week is also in November. It is a special week for children to enjoy reading good books. Good books can be read all year long. But Book Week is a week to promote reading and books. So read a good book for Book Week!

Questions: Creative Comprehension—Responding Emotionally

1. What do you like best about Thanksgiving?

____

____

____

2. Of all the books you have read, which ones did you like best?

____

____

____

Let's Write a Letter

Name ____________________

Biography: Squanto

Squanto was a Native American Indian. No one is sure when he was born. But he was taken to England in 1605.

Squanto lived in England until 1614. He probably learned how to speak English while he was there. In 1614, he was taken back to America.

Squanto met the Pilgrims at Plymouth Colony in 1621. He became their friend. Because he could speak English, he could talk to them. And he could tell them what the other Indians were saying.

Squanto acted as a guide for the Pilgrims. He helped them get places they wanted to go. He also showed them how to plant corn. And he showed them where to fish.

The Pilgrims had a lot to be thankful for at the first Thanksgiving in 1621. Their crops had done well, and they had plenty of food to eat. Their friend Squanto had helped them in many ways.

Questions: Creative Comprehension—Responding Emotionally

1. Would you like to be a guide like Squanto was? Why or why not?

____

____

____

2. Pretend you are a guide today. Where would you take people? What would you show them? On the back of your paper, write about what you would do if you were a guide.

Name ____________________

NOVEMBER

Sunday	Monday	Tuesday	Wednesday	Thursday	Friday	Saturday

Name ____________________

Words to Use in Your Writing

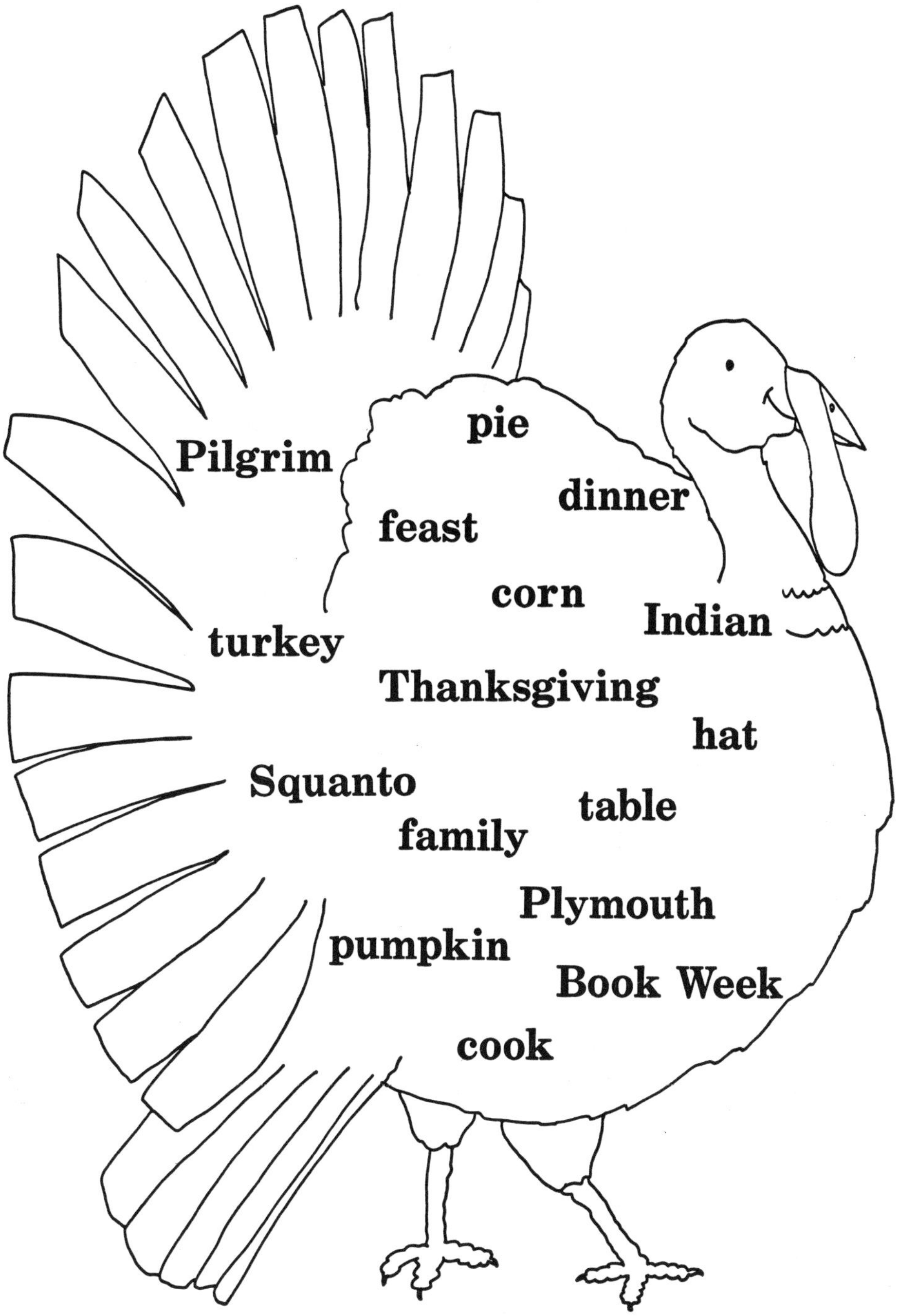

NOVEMBER

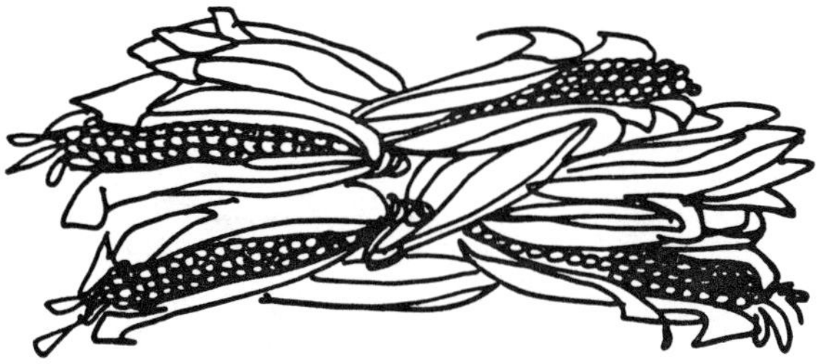

Name ______________________

Book Report

Title: ______________________

Author: ______________________

What the Book Was About:

____

____

____

____

____

____

____

My Reaction to the Book:

____

____

____

____

____

____

Name ____________________

Fiction: The Thanksgiving Feast

It was the day before Thanksgiving. Emily and Ryan's class was having a Thanksgiving feast. All the children brought good things to eat. There was lots and lots of food.

Emily and Ryan were helping with the food. They were going to make sure there was enough for everyone. As they worked, more and more children brought food.

Soon there was so much food that there was no place to put it all! There was more food than their class could eat. There was enough for three classes!

Emily and Ryan told their teacher there was too much food. Their teacher called all the children together. "We have too much food," she said. "What should we do?"

Questions: Inferential Comprehension—
Drawing Conclusions and Predicting Outcomes

1. Why is there too much food?

2. What will the children do with all the food?

Name ______________________

Play: The School Fair

Characters: Kathy, Linda, Pat, Girls, Chad, Chuck, John, Boys

Props: four school desks; four handwritten signs: (1) Go Fishing, (2) Guess a Number, (3) Tape the Nose on the Bear, and (4) Prizes; one "fishing pole" (a stick with a string and a paperclip hook); six handmade paper fish; one picture of a bear drawn on paper; one bear's nose drawn on paper; one cloth for a blindfold; one stuffed teddy bear; two or three other things for prizes

(The four desks are set up like tables at a fair.)

Table 1: Kathy is standing behind it. It has the sign "Go Fishing" taped to it. It has the fishing pole on it.

Table 2: Chuck is standing behind it. It has the sign "Guess a Number" taped to it.

Table 3: Chad is standing behind it. It has the sign "Tape the Nose on the Bear" taped to it. It has the drawing of a bear near it. On the table is the drawing of a bear's nose with tape on the back.

Table 4: John is standing behind it. It has the sign "Prizes" taped to it. It has the stuffed teddy bear and two or three other things on it.)

Girls: *It is the day of the big school fair. Tables are set up in the gym. All the children in the school are at the fair.*

Linda: What do you want to do first, Pat?

Pat: I think I want to go fishing. I'd love to win a teddy bear. Maybe I can catch a fish and win a teddy bear.

(Linda and Pat walk up to the "Go Fishing" table.)

Kathy: Hi, Linda and Pat. Would you like to try to catch a fish? Maybe you'll win something.

Linda: Pat wants to win a teddy bear.

Kathy: OK, Pat. Here's the fishing pole. Maybe you'll catch a fish and win a teddy bear.

(Kathy gives the pole to Pat. Pat tries to catch a fish. She can't catch one.)

Kathy: Well, you didn't catch a fish this time. Maybe you will next time.

Boys: *Pat wanted to win a bear. But she didn't win a bear. Poor Pat!*

Linda: What do you want to do next, Pat?

Pat: I want to play guess a number. Maybe I can guess the secret number and win a teddy bear.

(Linda and Pat walk up to the "Guess a Number" table.)

Chuck: Hi, Linda and Pat. Would you like to try to guess the secret number? Maybe you'll win something.

Linda: Pat wants to win a teddy bear.

Chuck: OK, Pat. Guess a number. Maybe you'll guess the secret number and win a teddy bear.

Pat: I guess the number 12. Is the secret number 12?

Chuck: No, it's not. You didn't guess it this time. Maybe you will next time.

Girls: *Pat wanted to win a bear. But she didn't win a bear. Poor Pat!*

Linda: What do you want to do now, Pat?

Pat: I want to try to tape the nose on the bear. Maybe I can tape on the bear's nose and win a teddy bear.

(Linda and Pat walk up to the "Tape the Nose on the Bear" table.)

Chad: Hi, Linda and Pat. Would you like to try to tape the nose on the bear? Maybe you'll win something.

Linda: Pat wants to win a teddy bear.

Chad: OK, Pat. Put on the blindfold.

(Linda and Chad help Pat put on the blindfold.)

Chad: Here is the bear's nose.

(Chad gives the bear's nose with tape on the back to Pat.)

Chad: Now see if you can tape the nose on the bear.

(Pat tries to tape the nose on the bear. Chad and Linda help her so that she tapes the nose in the right place. Then they help her take off the blindfold.)

Linda: You did it! You did it! You taped the nose on the bear!

Chad: You sure did. You may go to the "Prizes" table and pick out your prize.

(Linda and Pat walk up to the "Prizes table.)

John: Hi, Linda and Pat. Would you like to pick out a prize?

Linda: Pat would like a teddy bear.

Pat: Yes, I would! I'd really like a teddy bear.

John: OK. Here is a nice teddy bear. Would you like this one?

(John gives the teddy bear to Pat.)

Pat: Oh, thank you! I really like my bear!

Boys: *Pat wanted to win a bear. And she did win a bear. Proud Pat!*

Name ____________________

My Journal

Name ______________________________

My Poem

____

____

____

____

____

____

____

____

____

____

____

____

____

____

____

____

____

Name ____________________

Puzzle Page: Word Hunt

Directions: Look for these words and circle them when you find them: cook, corn, dinner, family, feast, hat, Indian, pie, Pilgrim, Plymouth, pumpkin, Squanto, table, Thanksgiving, turkey.

P	R	T	H	A	N	K	S	G	I	V	I	N	G
Y	G	F	K	M	D	R	W	I	O	D	H	E	C
Q	W	D	S	Q	U	A	N	T	O	R	A	O	P
U	Y	G	K	B	X	P	M	R	S	X	T	R	I
P	T	C	O	R	N	T	C	V	P	L	E	U	L
L	J	K	B	R	T	U	R	K	E	Y	P	R	G
Y	Y	R	B	C	V	K	E	M	I	O	U	D	R
M	O	I	W	F	E	A	S	T	R	V	M	P	I
O	M	N	M	R	S	T	A	B	L	E	P	C	M
U	N	D	B	A	Z	P	H	J	M	R	K	I	B
T	B	I	C	O	O	K	J	L	U	K	I	K	P
H	U	A	R	F	A	M	I	L	Y	P	N	E	I
P	T	N	J	L	M	S	D	F	K	R	Y	Q	E
R	S	D	C	V	I	D	I	N	N	E	R	Q	X

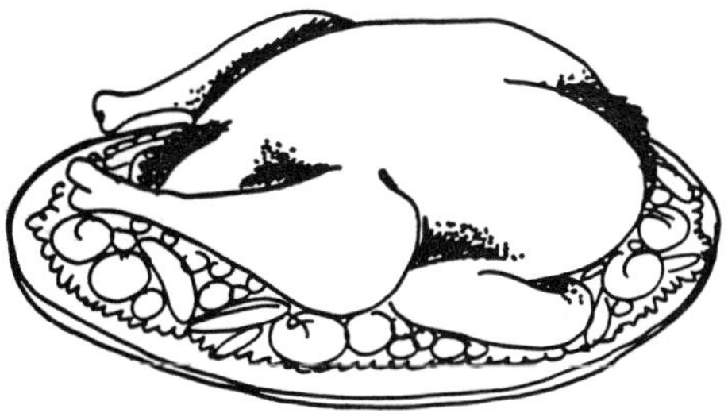

Name ______________________________

Just for Fun: Letter Squares

Directions: Write the missing letters in the squares to spell these words: cook, corn, dinner, family, feast, hat, Indian, pie, Pilgrim, Plymouth, pumpkin, Squanto, table, Thanksgiving, turkey. Then write the words on the lines below the squares.

1. T h □ n k s g □ v □ n g

____

2. P □ l g r □ m

____

3. S q u □ n t □

____

4. t □ b l □

____

5. f □ m □ l y

____

6. p □ □

____

7. c □ r n

____

8. P l y m □ □ t h

____

9. h □ t

____

10. I n d □ □ n

____

11. t □ r k □ y

____

12. d □ n n □ r

____

13. p □ m p k □ n

____

14. c □ □ k

____

15. f □ □ s t

____

Name ________________________________

Story Starter: Talking Books

It is Book Week. You and a friend are at the library. It is almost time for the library to close. Most people have gone home. Suddenly, all the books start talking. Each one is telling its own story. You run from book to book trying to hear all the stories at once! What happens next? Write about it.

Name ____________________

Following Directions: How to Make a Lunch Bag Turkey

You can make a turkey out of a lunch bag. Read to find out how to do it.

First, stuff sheets of newspaper into the lunch bag. When it is almost full, put a rubber band around the open end.

Next, make a turkey head out of paper. Tape the head to the bottom of the lunch bag.

Now you are ready to make tail feathers. Cut feathers from paper of different colors. Staple the paper feathers near the rubber band.

If you want to, you can paint your turkey with tempera paint. Or you can leave it like it is. Either way, it will look great on your table at Thanksgiving!

Questions: Literal Comprehension—Recalling Sequence

1. What do you do after you stuff newspaper into the bag?

____

____

____

2. After you tape on the turkey's head, what do you do?

____

____

____

Name ________________________

Thinking/Writing Page: Use Your Imagination

Pretend that for Book Week, you get to have a book written just for you. Use your imagination and tell what the book should be about. Who are the characters in the book, and what do they do? Write about the book you would like to have written.

____

____

____

____

____

____

____

____

____

____

____

____

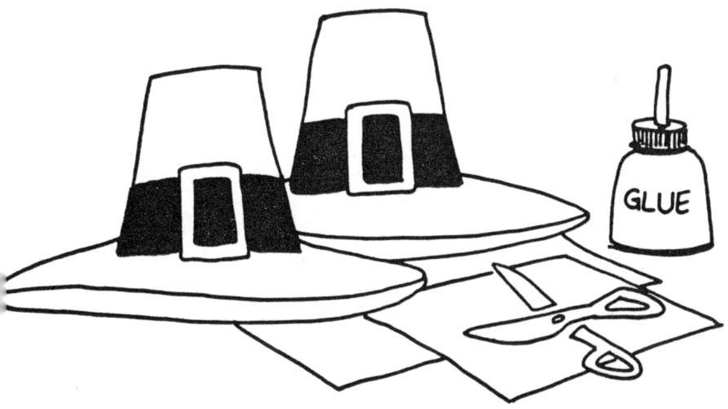

Name ____________________

Fantasy: Eating with the Pilgrims

Mike and Tim were sitting at Tim's kitchen table. They had just made some Pilgrim hats. They were going to wear them on Thanksgiving. They both put on the hats they made.

"I wish I could have been at the first Thanksgiving," said Mike.

"So do I," said Tim.

Just then, both boys felt funny. They felt as if they were flying through the air. When they landed, they were sitting at a wooden table. Pilgrims and Indians were sitting at the table with them.

"Hi!" said Mike. "Is it time to eat?"

"We've been eating for three days," said one of the Pilgrims. "But there is still a lot of food left. Help yourself. Then you can play some games with the other children."

When they finished eating, Mike and Tim took off their hats. Then both boys felt funny. They felt as if they were flying through the air. When they landed, they were sitting at Tim's kitchen table. The things they had used to make their hats were still on the table.

Question: Critical Comprehension—Distinguishing Fantasy from Reality

1. How do you know this story could not really happen?

____

____

____

____

READING AWARD

______________________________ Is Presented

With This Award For:

____

____

____

Signed ______________________

Date ______________________

DECEMBER

MY WISH FOR THE WORLD

Name ______________________________

Rebus Story: Buying Gifts

 Leslie and  Connie had been saving their money for a long time. They kept it in their  bank. They were going to buy  presents with the money.

The girls went to the  store near their  house. They looked around at all the things in the  store.

"Here is a  scarf that mom would like," said  Leslie. "OK," said  Connie. "I think she'll like that. Do you think dad would like a  hat?"

"Oh, yes," said  Leslie. "He's been saying that his head gets cold in the winter."

"Do you think grandma and grandpa would like  books?" asked  Connie. "There is a bookstore down the street."

"Yes," said  Leslie. "Let's go there after we pay for the  scarf and  hat."

Questions: Literal Comprehension—Recalling Details

1. What are the girls going to buy for their mom and dad?

____

2. What are they going to buy for their grandma and grandpa?

____

Handwriting Practice

Name ________________________

Name ____________________

Nonfiction: December

December is a time for holidays. Christmas is on December 25. It is a time for being with family and friends. It is a time for giving gifts.

Many people send Christmas cards in December. Sometimes they write notes on the cards. In the notes they tell their friends what they have been doing.

In December, Christmas carols are often sung. Many schools have programs where children sing Christmas carols. Sometimes they sing around a Christmas tree.

Hanukkah also begins in December. Hanukkah is a Jewish festival that lasts for eight days. It is also called the Festival of Lights.

December is a special month because of the holidays. Some people think it is the best month of the year!

Questions: Creative Comprehension—Responding Emotionally

1. What do you like best about December?

____

____

2. Think about the best time you have ever had during the holidays. Write about what you did. Use the back of your paper if you need to.

____

____

Let's Write a Letter

Name ____________________

Biography: Thomas Edison

Thomas Edison was born in Ohio in 1847. He has been called the world's greatest inventor. He invented over 1,100 different things.

One of Edison's inventions was a small electric lightbulb. Other people had made large electric lights. But Edison wanted a small light that people could use in their homes. He tried putting different things inside the bulb to make it work. He even tried using red hair from a friend's beard! Finally, in 1879, he made a small lightbulb that worked.

Another of Edison's inventions was the record player. At first, he recorded voices. Later, he recorded music.

Edison worked very hard all his life. Once he was working on a battery and couldn't get it to work. He did 10,000 different experiments and none of them worked. He said, "Why, I have not failed. I've just found 10,000 ways that won't work."

Thomas Edison died in New Jersey in 1931. He was eighty-four years old. When you see pretty colored lights during the holidays, you will know who invented the electric lightbulb.

Questions: Creative Comprehension—Responding Emotionally

1. Would you like to be an inventor like Thomas Edison? Why or why not?

____

____

2. If you were an inventor, what would you invent? On the back of your paper, write about something you would like to invent. Then draw a picture of your invention and give it a name.

Name ______________________

DECEMBER

Sunday	Monday	Tuesday	Wednesday	Thursday	Friday	Saturday

Name ____________________

Words to Use in Your Writing

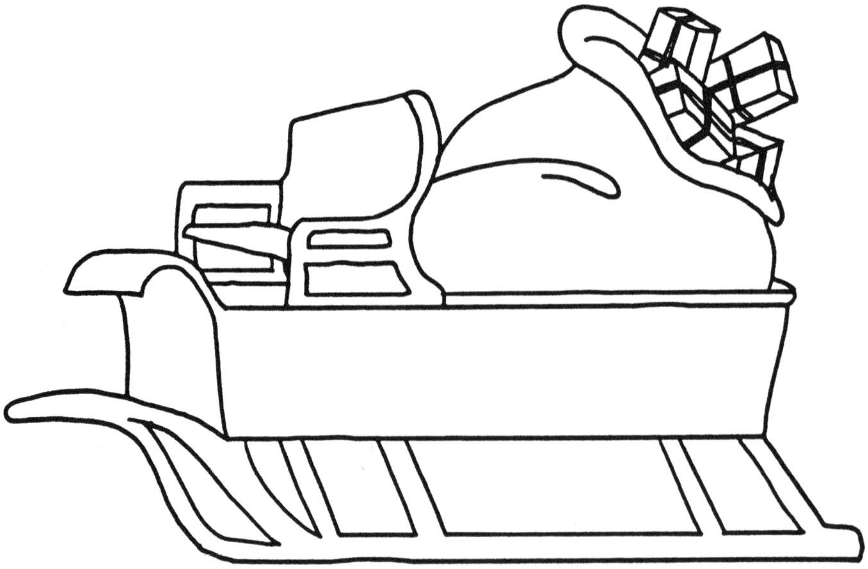

DECEMBER

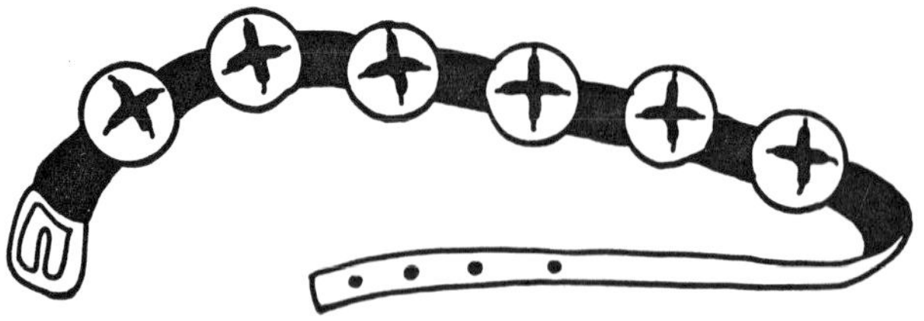

Name ______________________

Book Report

Title: ______________________

Author: ______________________

What the Book Was About:

____

____

____

____

____

____

____

My Reaction to the Book:

____

____

____

____

____

____

Name ____________________

Fiction: Making Holiday Treats

Ryan was at Emily's house. They were making treats for the holidays. They made cookies and candy.

Ryan and Emily made the cookies in many pretty shapes. They used a cookie cutter. Then Emily put the cookies in the oven. After that, Emily and Ryan went into the living room.

"Let's play a game while the cookies are baking," said Emily.

"OK," said Ryan. "What do you want to play?"

"Let's play a word game," said Emily. "Let's see how many words we can make with the letters in the word *holidays.* The one who thinks of the most words wins."

So Emily and Ryan started to write down the words they could make. Just then, they heard a loud noise. The smoke alarm in the kitchen was making an awful sound. They ran into the kitchen to see what was going on.

Questions: Inferential Comprehension—
Drawing Conclusions and Predicting Outcomes

1. What made the smoke alarm go off?

____

____

____

2. What will Emily and Ryan do next?

____

____

____

Name ________________

Play: The Holiday Mural

Characters: Anne, Julie, Laura, Girls, Greg, Jake, Zach, Boys

Props: one very large sheet of white paper for a mural; one set of colored markers or crayons

(The white paper is taped to a wall or chalkboard. The people in the play will draw on the paper.)

Girls: *It is time to make the holiday mural. What will they draw? What will they draw?*

(Anne has a green marker or crayon in her hand.)

Anne: I think we should start with a tree. A holiday mural should have a tree.

Greg: Yes, we need a tree. Draw a tree for us, Anne.

(Anne draws a pine tree in the middle of the mural.)

Greg: Wow! That's good! I like the tree you drew, Anne.

Anne: Thank you. Would you like to draw some decorations on the tree?

(Greg picks up three or four markers or crayons of different colors.)

Greg: Yes, I'll draw some decorations.

(Greg draws decorations on the tree.)

Boys: *Now they have a decorated tree. But they need something else. What will they draw? What will they draw?*

Julie: I think we need some presents. A holiday mural should have presents.

Jake: Yes, we need presents. Draw some presents for us, Julie.

(Julie draws some presents on one side of the tree.)

Jake: Wow! That's good! I like the presents you drew, Julie.

Julie: Thank you. Would you like to draw some name tags on the presents?

(Jake picks up a red marker or crayon.)

Jake: Yes, I'll draw some name tags.

(Jake draws name tags on the presents.)

Girls: *Now they have a decorated tree. And they have presents with name tags. But they need something else. What will they draw? What will they draw?*

Zach: I think we need a table where people can eat. A holiday mural should have a table.

Laura: Yes, we need a table. Draw a table for us, Zach.

(Zach draws a big table beside the tree.)

Laura: Wow! That's good! I like the table you drew, Zach.

Zach: Thank you. Would you like to draw some food on the table?

(Laura picks up three or four markers or crayons of different colors.)

Laura: Yes, I'll draw some food.

(Laura draws some food on the table.)

Boys: *Now they have a decorated tree. And they have presents with name tags and a table full of food. They have everything they need. What a nice holiday mural!*

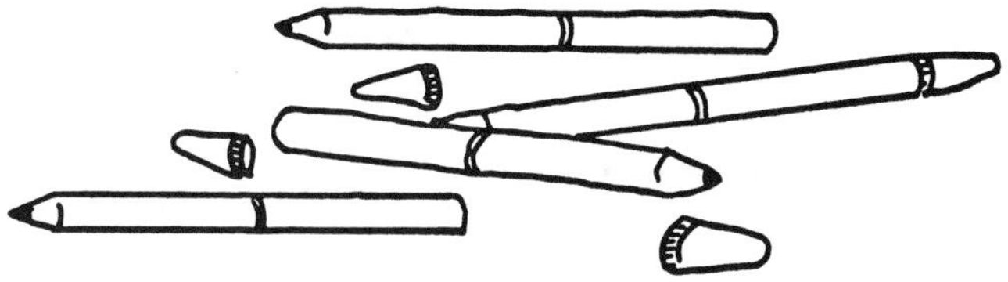

Name ______________________

My Journal

____

Name ____________________

My Poem

Name ______________________________

Puzzle Page: Word Seek

Directions: Look for these words and circle them when you find them: candle, candy, cards, Christmas, elves, gifts, Hanukkah, lights, ornaments, party, reindeer, Santa, sleigh, stocking, tree, wreath.

P	W	O	R	N	A	M	E	N	T	S	R	W	Q
R	V	J	I	D	C	R	G	I	F	T	S	X	L
C	M	T	R	E	E	R	F	G	H	H	E	J	S
A	B	G	H	X	L	K	U	E	A	A	D	F	T
N	M	C	J	S	A	N	T	A	T	N	U	I	O
D	I	H	M	J	K	D	S	Y	R	U	O	R	C
L	U	R	C	E	L	V	E	S	T	K	Q	E	K
E	H	I	O	T	G	F	V	I	L	K	O	I	I
W	S	S	C	A	R	D	S	M	I	A	T	N	N
U	T	T	B	M	N	K	E	L	G	H	W	D	G
R	J	M	M	P	A	R	T	Y	H	I	O	E	R
R	Q	A	C	A	N	D	Y	W	T	M	P	E	V
T	G	S	Q	W	B	V	M	N	S	J	I	R	U
W	R	E	A	T	H	R	V	S	L	E	I	G	H

Name ____________________

Just for Fun: Name the Pictures

Directions: Under each picture, write the word that names the picture. Choose from the words in the word box below.

1. ____________

2. ____________

3. ____________

4. ____________

5. ____________

6. ____________

7. ____________

8. ____________

9. ____________

10. ____________

11. ____________

12. ____________

candle candy cane
card elf ornament
present reindeer Santa
sleigh stocking
tree wreath

Name ______________________

Story Starter: The School Program

Your school is having a holiday program. You are going to sing a song by yourself. Many people have come to hear you sing. Soon it is your turn. You open your mouth, but no sound comes out. Everyone is waiting. What happens next? Write about it.

Name ______________________________

Following Directions: How to Make Holiday Cookies

To make holiday cookies, you will need these things:

2 cups flour	2/3 cup shortening
1/2 teaspoon salt	2 eggs
2 teaspoons baking powder	1 teaspoon vanilla
2/3 cup sugar	

Sift together the flour, salt, and baking powder. Set this aside.

In a bowl, mix the sugar, shortening, and eggs. Mix them all together until they are creamy.

Next, add the flour mixture to the sugar and shortening mixture. Add the vanilla, too. Then mix everything all together.

Now put the bowl in the refrigerator. Leave it there for two hours. Chilling the dough will make it easier to work with.

When the dough is chilled, set the oven at 375°. Then grease your cookie sheet.

Now it is time to make the cookies. Wash your hands and put a little flour on them. Next, pick up a little dough, roll it in a ball, and put it on the cookie sheet. Then dip the bottom of a glass in flour and press the glass down on the cookie.

Keep making balls of dough and put them in rows on the cookie sheet. After you make each ball, press down on it with the bottom of the glass. When the cookie sheet is full, put it in the oven until the cookies are done (ten to fifteen minutes). Then take the cookie sheet out of the oven. After the cookies are cool, you can decorate them with colored icing.

Questions: Literal Comprehension—Recalling Sequence

1. What do you do after you sift the flour, salt, and baking powder?

____

2. After you roll the dough in a ball, what do you do?

____

Name ____________________

Thinking/Writing Page: Just Suppose

Just suppose you have a great deal of money. You can buy anything you want to buy as long as you buy it for other people. Who will you buy gifts for? What will you buy them? Write about it.

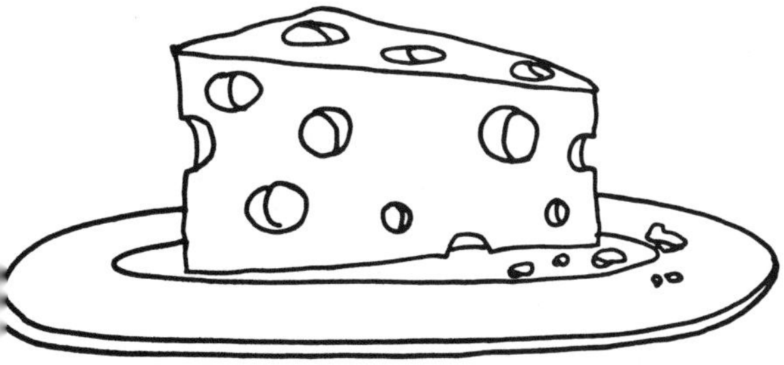

Name ____________________

Fantasy: Changing Size

Tim and Mike had just read a story called *The Night Before Christmas.* "I like that story," said Tim.

"So do I," said Mike. "I liked where it said, *Not a creature was stirring, not even a mouse.*"

"I wonder what it feels like to be as small as a mouse," said Tim.

"We can't be as small as a mouse," said Mike. "But we can eat cheese like they do. Here, have some cheese."

So both boys ate some cheese. As soon as they ate the cheese, they started to feel funny. They both got smaller and smaller and smaller.

"That must have been magic cheese," said Mike. "We are both as small as a mouse!"

"This is neat!" said Tim. "Now we can go all over the house. We're small enough to go anywhere!"

Tim and Mike had a great time running and playing all over the house. They went under the beds and on top of the refrigerator. They went everywhere!

"Oh, no! I think the magic is going away," said Tim. "I'm getting big again."

"So am I," said Mike. "But maybe it's just as well. My mom will be home any minute now!"

Question: Critical Comprehension—Distinguishing Fantasy from Reality

1. Do you think this story could really happen? Why or why not? Write your answer on the back of your paper.

READING AWARD

______________________________ Is Presented

With This Award For:

____

____

____

Signed ______________________

Date ______________________

JANUARY

THINGS I LIKE TO DO

Name ____________________

Rebus Story: The Snowy Day

When  Leslie and  Connie woke up, it was snowing. It had been snowing all night. The roads were covered with snow. There was so much snow that the girls did not have school that day.

"Let's go out and play after breakfast," said  Connie.

"OK," said  Leslie.

After breakfast, the girls each put on a  coat. Then they each put on a warm  hat and a pair of  boots. Just before they went outside, they put on warm  gloves.

When they got outside, the girls started to build a  snowman. After they built the  snowman, they built a  snow woman. Then they built a  snow baby.

"I like our  snow family," said  Connie. "Let's see if Mom will come out and take a picture of it!"

Questions: Literal Comprehension—Recalling Details

1. What did the girls put on before they went outside?

____

2. What did they build with the snow?

____

Handwriting Practice

Name ______________________

Name ____________________

Nonfiction: January

The new year begins in January. New Year's Day is on January 1. On that day, there are football games and parades. Many people watch them on television.

In most places, January is a cold month. Many people get snow in January. When it snows, boys and girls can build snow people. They can also throw snowballs!

Some children ride on sleds in the snow. They find a hill and pull their sled to the top of it. Then they slide down the hill on the sled!

When children play outside in the snow, they have to wear warm clothes. They wear coats, hats, and gloves. And they wear boots to keep their feet dry and warm. Sometimes they have so much fun playing in the snow that they don't even know it's cold outside!

Questions: Creative Comprehension—Responding Emotionally

1. What are some of the things you like to do in January?

____

____

2. Think about the most fun you ever had on a winter day. Write about what you did that day. Use the back of your paper if you need to.

____

____

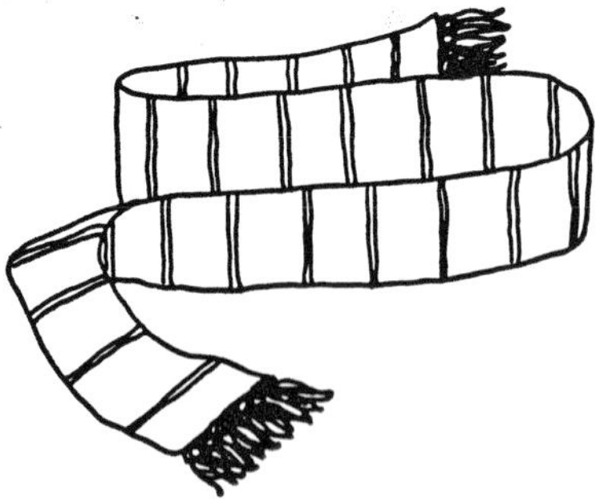

Let's Write a Letter

Name ______________________

Biography: Martin Luther King, Jr.

Martin Luther King, Jr. was born in Georgia on January 15, 1929. His father was a Baptist minister. His grandfather was a minister, too.

Martin was a good student. He went to college when he was only fifteen. After he finished college, he became a minister.

Martin Luther King worked hard to help other people. He led marches to help give black people the right to vote. He also worked to help the poor. He wanted all people to have jobs and a decent place to live.

The March on Washington was held in 1963. More than 250,000 people were there. They heard King make his "I Have a Dream" speech. The next year, he was given the Nobel Peace Prize for his work.

In 1968, King was in Memphis, Tennessee to help some people who were on strike. On April 4, he was shot and killed. People remember him for all the things he did to help others. Each year in January, there is a holiday in honor of his birthday.

Questions: Creative Comprehension—Responding Emotionally

1. Do you think it is important to help other people? Why or why not?

____

____

____

2. What things can you do to help others? On the back of your paper, write about what you can do.

Name ____________________

JANUARY

Sunday	Monday	Tuesday	Wednesday	Thursday	Friday	Saturday

Name ______________________________

Words to Use in Your Writing

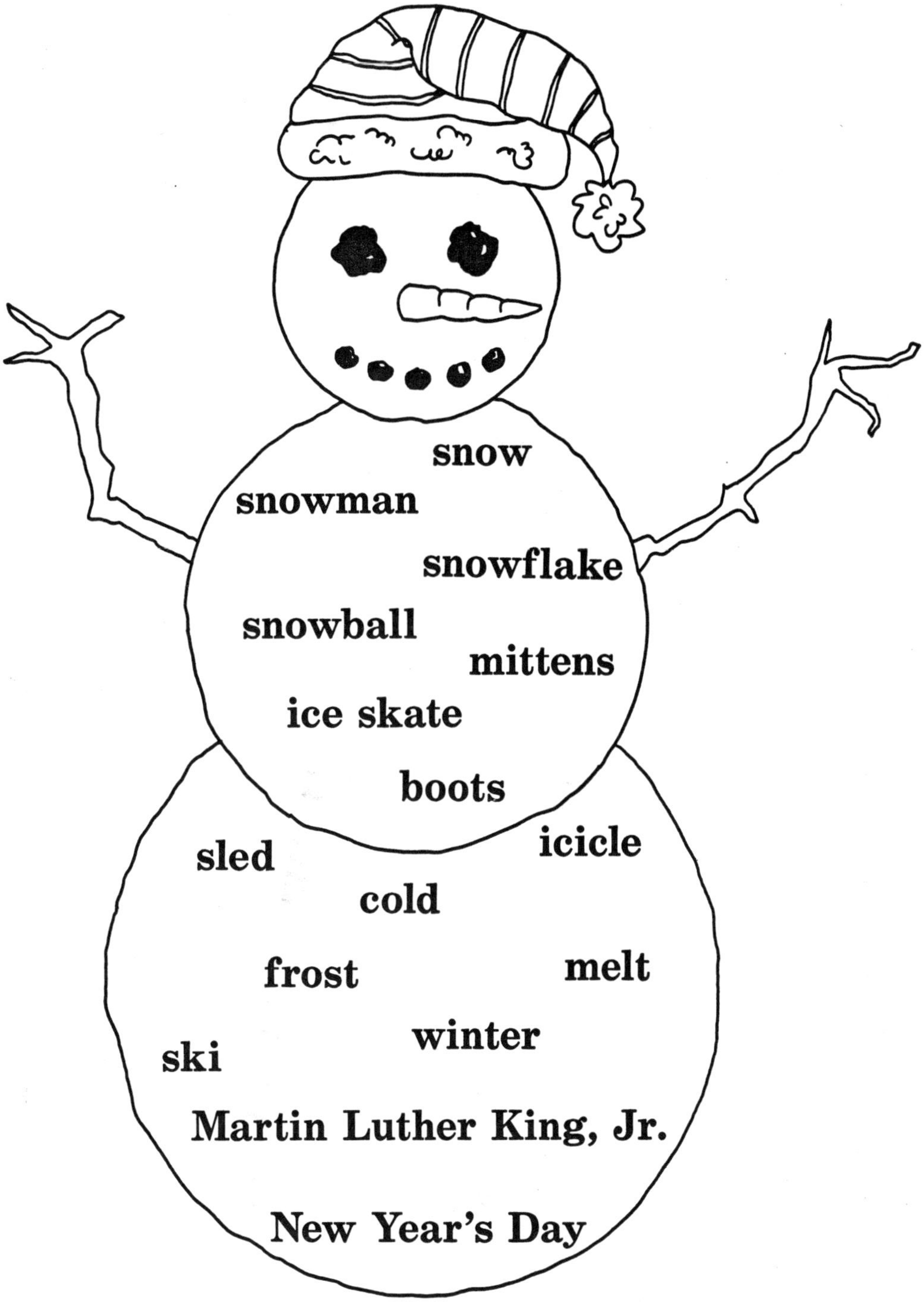

JANUARY

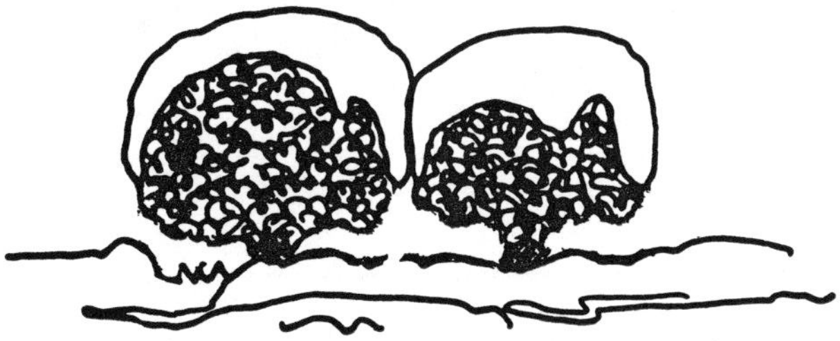

Name ______________________

Book Report

Title: ______________________

Author: ______________________

What the Book Was About:

____

____

____

____

____

____

____

My Reaction to the Book:

____

____

____

____

____

____

Name ______________________________

Fiction: A Good Book

Emily was at Ryan's house. It was a very cold day. Ryan's dad had built a fire in the fireplace.

Emily and Ryan were reading a book by the fire. The book was about a boy and girl who went outside on a cold day.

The boy and girl in the book built a snowman. They put a hat on his head. They put some mittens on him. Then they used rocks to make his eyes, nose, and mouth.

After they built the snowman, the boy and girl went inside and read some books. While they were inside, it got much warmer.

The next day, it got even warmer. The sun was very hot. It got warmer, warmer, and warmer.

Questions: Inferential Comprehension—
Predicting Outcomes and Drawing Conclusions

1. What will happen next in the book Emily and Ryan are reading?

____

____

____

2. Do you think Emily and Ryan like to read books? Why or why not?

____

____

____

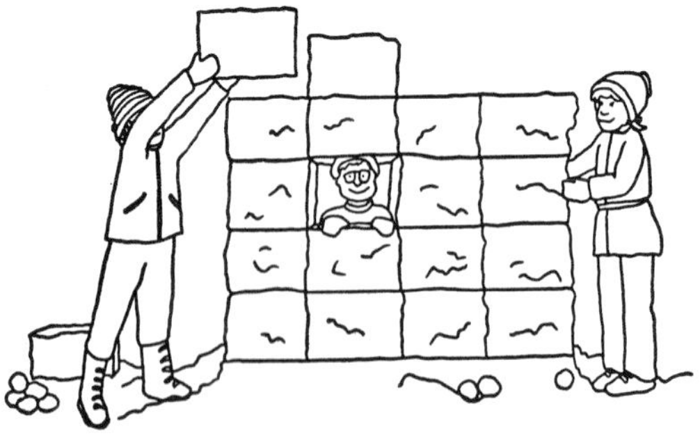

Name ____________________

Play:
The Big Snow

Characters:	David	Bonnie	Props:	six winter jackets
	Matt	Cindy		six pairs of gloves
	Ty	Gail		one inflated inner tube
	Boys	Girls		one sign that says "One Month Later"

Boys: *All winter long, children waited for a big snow. But all they got was rain, rain, and more rain.*

David: When is it going to snow? We haven't had a good snow yet this year!

Matt: Winter will soon be over. Maybe we aren't going to get any snow this year. Maybe all we're going to get is rain!

Ty: We have snow every winter. Maybe it's just late this year. I have my inner tube ready for when it does snow! (Ty holds up his inner tube.)

Girls: *Even though there is no snow, children still hope there will be. Some children are trying on their winter jackets.*

Bonnie: How do you like my jacket? I think it will be plenty warm for playing in the snow.

Cindy: Your jacket looks really warm. Here's the one I'm going to wear. How do you like it?

Gail: Both of you look nice in your jackets. They should keep you warm when we finally get snow. How do you like my jacket? I think my jacket should be plenty warm, too.

Boys: *The boys have their inner tube ready. And the girls have their jackets ready. But still there isn't any snow.*

(Someone holds up the sign that says "One Month Later.")

Girls: *When everyone woke up, they looked out their windows. It had been snowing all night! There was snow everywhere! Children put on their jackets and gloves. Then they went outside to play in the snow.*

David: Hi, Matt! Are you ready to go sliding down the big hill?

Matt: I sure am! We can use Ty's inner tube. Here he comes! I see him now!

(Ty is walking toward David and Matt. He is carrying his inner tube.)

Ty: Hi, guys! Let's go slide down the hill!

Boys: *The boys start toward the big hill. On the way, they walk past where the girls are building a snow fort.*

Bonnie: Hi there! Do you want to help us build our fort?

Cindy: We could use some help. We almost have it done.

Gail: After we finish the fort, we can all go slide down the big hill together.

Girls: *The boys stay and work on the fort. When the fort is finished, they all have a big snowball fight.*

Cindy: That was fun! I like to throw snowballs!

Bonnie: I want to make something else out of the snow. What can we make?

David: I know what we can make! Let's make a giant Mickey Mouse!

Boys: *They go to the backyard where there is plenty of snow. They work and work. They build a giant Mickey Mouse out of snow.*

Ty: Hey, everybody! We still haven't gotten to slide down the big hill!

Matt: That's right! We've been having so much fun that I almost forgot!

Gail: I'll get my inner tube, too. We can all take turns going down the hill.

Girls: *They walk to the big hill at the end of their street. Then they slide down the hill many, many times. At lunchtime, they all go home for lunch. Then they go back to the hill and play all afternoon.*

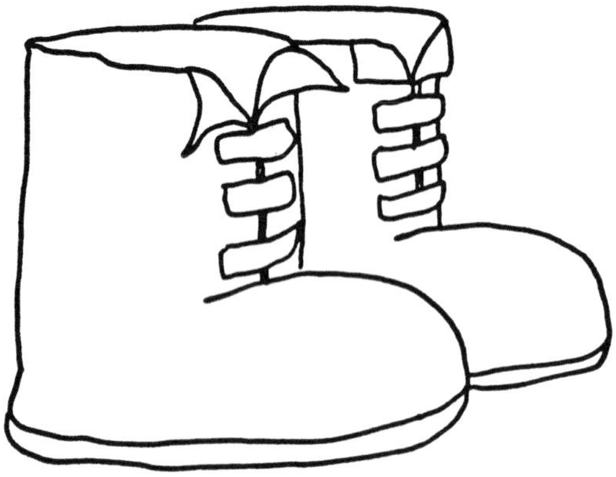

Name

My Journal

Name ______________________________

My Poem

____

Name ____________________

Puzzle Page: Find the Words

Directions: Look for these words and circle them when you find them: boots, cold, frost, ice, icicle, melt, mittens, skate, ski, sled, snow, snowball, snowflake, snowman, winter.

Y	S	N	O	W	F	L	A	K	E	R	P	I	R
E	F	G	B	X	K	W	Q	I	V	X	C	L	J
C	S	F	D	M	I	T	T	E	N	S	M	O	S
O	R	H	T	I	O	P	R	E	D	B	X	V	N
L	G	S	M	B	V	F	R	O	S	T	X	K	O
D	B	N	T	B	I	E	F	H	K	L	S	G	W
D	X	O	R	O	M	K	D	X	S	W	K	P	M
Y	M	W	P	O	V	S	L	E	D	T	A	H	A
S	Q	B	W	T	O	R	F	B	N	M	T	J	N
K	J	A	A	S	M	S	N	O	W	T	E	R	F
I	H	L	J	L	P	O	Y	I	T	V	B	M	R
K	X	L	Q	I	C	E	W	M	E	L	T	S	A
E	C	V	J	K	R	S	D	O	U	A	Y	R	J
W	I	N	T	E	R	C	I	C	I	C	L	E	X

Name ______________________

Just for Fun: Make Compound Words

Directions: The name of each picture is a compound word that contains the word *snow*. For the second part of each word, choose from these words: ball, bird, drift, fall, fence, flake, man, mobile, plow, shoe, suit, tire. Then finish each compound word by writing the correct word on each line.

1. ______________ 2. ______________ 3. ______________

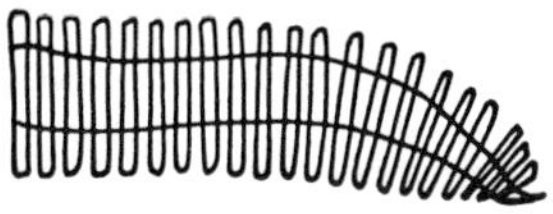

4. ______________ 5. ______________ 6. ______________

7. ______________ 8. ______________ 9. ______________

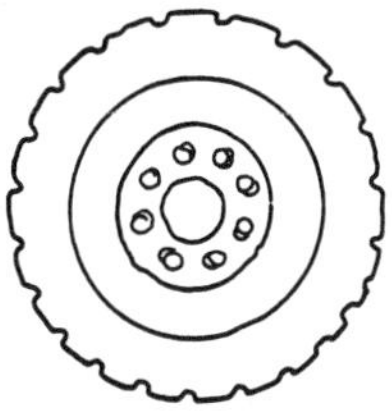
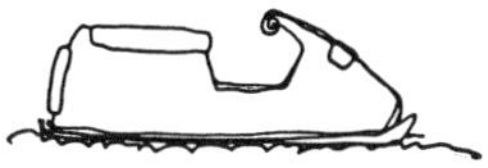

10. ______________ 11. ______________ 12. ______________

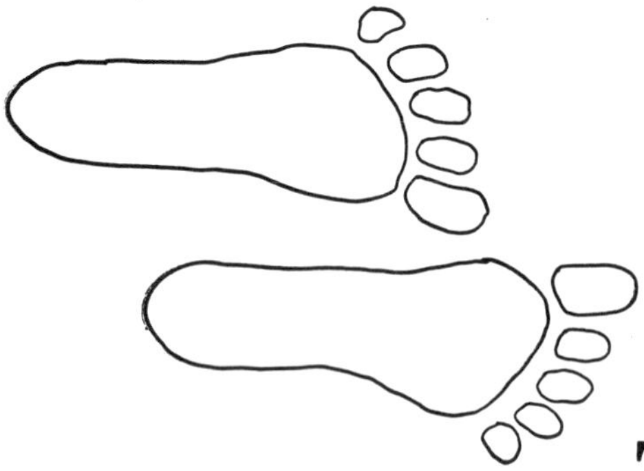

Name ______________________

Story Starter: The Big Snowman

You and your friend are walking in the woods. It has been snowing. Suddenly, right in front of you, is a *big* snowman. It is the kind that people call Bigfoot. What happens next? Write about it.

Name ______________________________

Following Directions: How to Make Mini Snowflakes

You can make a pretty plastic snowflake. Read to find out how to do it.

Start with a sheet of clear plastic. It should be fairly heavy plastic. But it can be like the plastic your teacher writes on when she uses the overhead projector.

Draw a snowflake on the plastic with a blue or black marker. Your snowflake should be about two or three inches wide.

Next, cut out your snowflake. Then punch a hole in it. Use a hole punch to make a hole about 1/4 inch from the edge. Then put a 24-inch piece of yarn through the hole and tie the two ends of the yarn together.

Now your snowflake is ready to hang somewhere. You can even wear it for a necklace!

Questions: Literal Comprehension—Recalling Sequence

1. What do you do after you draw your snowflake?

____

____

2. After you punch a hole in your snowflake, what do you do?

____

____

Name ______________________________

Thinking/Writing Page: Imagine That

Imagine that you are standing outside. You are looking at a snowman you just built. Suddenly, the snowman starts to move. He is alive! What does he do? What do you do? Write about it.

Name ________________________________

Fantasy: Football Players

Mike and Tim were at Tim's house. They were watching a football game on television. It was New Year's Day.

"I wish I was big enough to play football on television," said Mike.

"So do I," said Tim. "We can't play football on television. But we can play here. Let's put on these helmets."

So Mike and Tim both put on football helmets. Right after that, they started to feel funny. They felt as if they were moving through the air. When they stopped, they were on a football field. They were playing in the football game they had been watching on television!

"Wow!" said Mike. "I have the ball! And all these players are coming at me! Tim, where are you?"

"Here I am, Mike," said Tim. "I'm open. Throw me the ball fast!"

Mike threw the football to Tim. Tim ran with the ball. He ran across the line. He made a touchdown!

Mike went over to where Tim was. They were both very happy, and tired. They went over to sit down. Then they both took off their helmets. Right after that, they started to feel funny. They felt as if they were moving through the air. When they stopped, they were at Tim's house.

"Did that really happen?" asked Mike.

"I don't think so," said Tim. "Maybe we dreamed it." Then Tim looked down at his feet. On his feet was a pair of football shoes.

Question: Critical Comprehension—Distinguishing Fantasy from Reality

1. Which parts of this story make you think the story could not really happen? Write your answer on the back of your paper.

READING AWARD

______________________________ **Is Presented**

With This Award For:

____

____

____

Signed ____________________

Date ____________________

FEBRUARY

LOVE IS . . .

Name ______________________________

Rebus Story: The Valentine Party

It was February 14—Valentine's Day.  Leslie and  Connie were on their way to a party.

 Leslie had on her new red  dress.  Connie had on her pretty white  dress. Both girls brought the valentines they had made.

When they got to the party,  Leslie and  Connie saw all their friends. They had brought valentines, too. Everyone passed out the valentines they brought for each other.

After all the valentines were passed out, it was time to eat. They ate  cake,  cookies, and  candy.  Leslie ate too much. She was afraid she would get a tummy ache!

When the party was over, everyone said good-bye to their friends. They all liked the valentines they had gotten, and they all had a good time.

Questions: Literal Comprehension—Recalling Details

1. When was the party?

____

2. What did they eat at the party?

____

Handwriting Practice

Name ______________________________

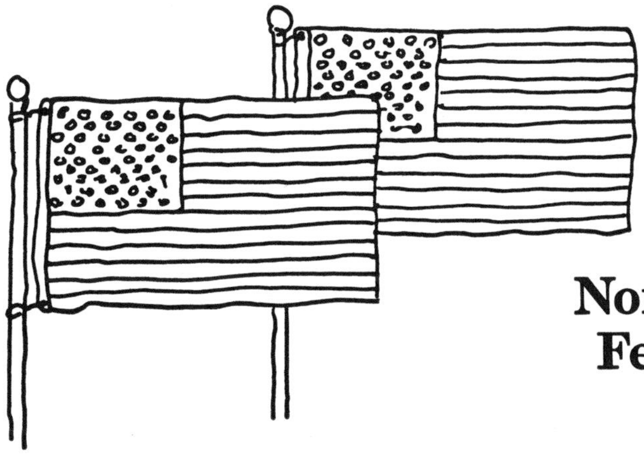

Name ________________________________

Nonfiction: February

The second day of February is Groundhog Day. There is a story about what a groundhog does on that day. If it sees its shadow when it comes out of its hole, winter will last six more weeks. If it does not see its shadow, warm weather will be coming soon.

February 14 is Valentine's Day. On that day, many people send cards to each other. There are often parties at school on that day.

Many, many years ago, there was a man in Italy named Valentine. Some people say he wrote a note and signed it *From Your Valentine.* This may have been the first valentine.

President's Day also comes in February. This is the day people honor George Washington and Abraham Lincoln. Both men were born in February.

Questions: Creative Comprehension—Responding Emotionally

1. What do you like most about Valentine's Day?

____

____

2. Write about someone you like very much. Be sure to tell why you like them. Use the back of your paper if you need to.

____

____

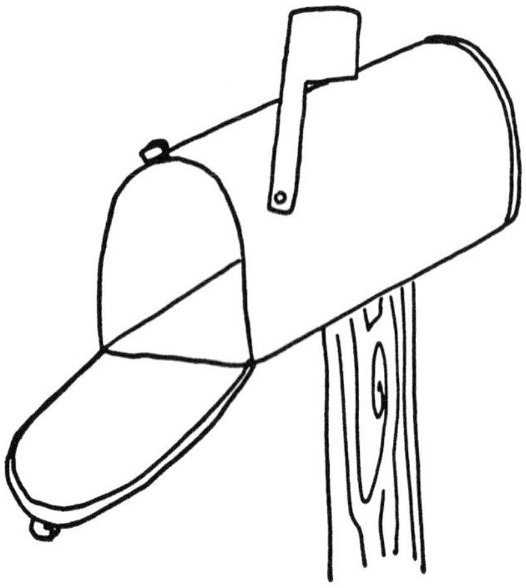

Let's Write a Letter

Name ____________________

Biography: George Washington and Abraham Lincoln

Both George Washington and Abraham Lincoln were born in February. Washington was born on February 22, 1732. Lincoln was born on February 12, 1809.

George Washington and Abraham Lincoln were famous presidents. Washington was the first president of the United States. Lincoln was the sixteenth president.

George Washington is often called "The Father of Our Country" since he was our first president. Abraham Lincoln is remembered because he freed the slaves.

George Washington died in 1799 at the age of sixty-seven. In 1865, Abraham Lincoln was shot and killed by John Wilkes Booth. He was fifty-six years old when he died.

Questions: Creative Comprehension—Responding Emotionally

1. Would you like to be president of the United States when you grow up? Why or why not?

____

____

____

____

2. If you were president, what kinds of things would you do? On the back of your paper, write about what you would do.

Name ______________________

FEBRUARY

Sunday	Monday	Tuesday	Wednesday	Thursday	Friday	Saturday

Name ______________________________

Words to Use in Your Writing

Valentine's Day
love
poem
hug
candy
card
happy
cookies
heart
valentine box
cupid
George Washington
Abraham Lincoln
present
President's Day
Groundhog Day

FEBRUARY

Be
Mine

Name ______________________

Book Report

Title: ______________________

Author: ______________________

What the Book Was About:

____

____

____

____

____

____

____

My Reaction to the Book:

____

____

____

____

____

____

Name ____________________

Fiction: Ryan's Valentines

Ryan and Emily were working on their valentines. They wrote all their friends' names on them.

The next day was Valentine's Day. Ryan and Emily took their valentines to school. Their class was going to have a party that afternoon.

When the class went to PE, Ryan left his valentines on his desk. When he got back from PE, his valentines were gone.

Everyone in the class looked for Ryan's valentines. They looked everywhere they could think of. But no one could find the valentines.

Questions: Inferential Comprehension—
Drawing Conclusions and Predicting Outcomes

1. What do you think happened to Ryan's valentines?

____

____

____

2. What do you think will happen next?

____

____

____

Name ________________________________

Play: Popping Corn

Characters:	Jay	Jane	Props:	one electric popcorn popper
	Tad	Joy		one bag of popcorn
	Todd	Lynn		one bottle of vegetable oil
	Boys	Girls		one measuring cup

Boys: *Everyone in the class has been working hard. They have done their work well. So their teacher is going to let them make popcorn.*

Jay: Oh, boy! We get to make popcorn! I'm so glad our teacher is going to let us make popcorn! Oh. How do you make popcorn?

Todd: Don't you know how to make popcorn?

Jay: I do know how. But not this way. My mom just puts the package in the microwave and it makes itself! I've never made popcorn in a popcorn popper!

Tad: Well, we'll show you how. But you'll have to be careful so you won't burn yourself. The popper gets really hot.

Girls: *So they are going to make popcorn. But they are going to be careful. Because the popper gets really hot!*

Jane: First, we put in the oil. We need one-fourth cup of oil. I'll pour the oil.

(Jane pours one-fourth cup of oil into the measuring cup. Then she pours the oil from the cup into the base of the popcorn popper.)

Joy: I'll get the popcorn. We need two-thirds cup of popcorn.

(Joy pours two-thirds cup of popcorn into the measuring cup. Then she pours the popcorn from the cup into the base of the popcorn popper.)

Lynn: Now we need to put the cover on and plug it in. I'll do that. (Lynn puts the cover on the popcorn popper. Then she plugs the cord into an outlet.)

Jay: It's not doing anything. Why isn't it popping?

Todd: It will. You just have to wait a while. The oil has to get hot first.

Boys: *So the oil and the popcorn are in the popper. But it's not popping yet. All they can do is wait, wait, wait.*

(Everyone waits. Soon the corn starts popping.)

Tad: Pop! There it goes! It's started popping!

Jane: Pop! Pop! Pop! More are popping now!

Joy: Wow! Lot's more are popping! Pop! Pop! Pop!

Lynn: Soon it will all be popped. Then we'll have popcorn!

(Everyone waits. Soon all the popcorn has popped.)

Jay: It's ready now! Let's get it out of there so we can eat it!

Todd: First our teacher has to turn the popper over. Then all the popcorn will be in the cover.

(The teacher turns over the popper. The popcorn is now in the cover.)

Jay: Now can we eat it? It's ready, isn't it?

Tad: No, not yet. It needs to cool a little. You might burn your mouth.

Jay: No I won't. I've waited too long. I'm ready even if it isn't.

(Jay picks up a piece of popcorn and puts it to his mouth.)

Jay: Ouch! It is hot! You were right. It does need to cool a little.

Girls: *So the popcorn is ready. It just has to cool. Then everyone can eat popcorn.*

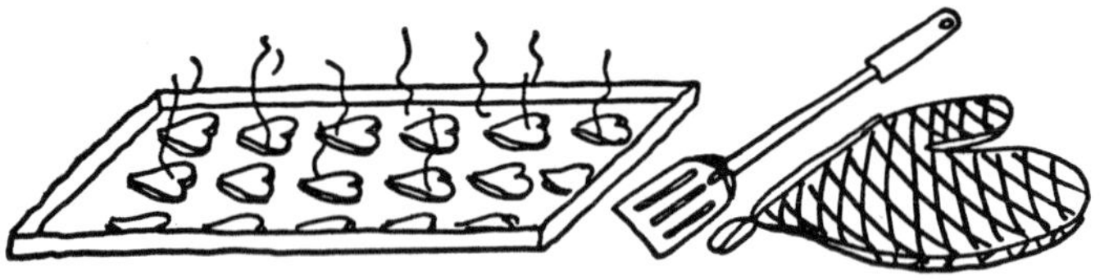

Name ______________________

My Journal

Name ______________________________

My Poem

Name ____________________

Puzzle Page: Word Search

Directions: Look for these words and circle them when you find them: candy, card, cookies, cupid, happy, heart, hug, Lincoln, love, poem, present, president, Valentine, Washington.

W	F	V	A	L	E	N	T	I	N	E	R	F	L
G	P	M	H	J	U	F	V	C	X	Q	I	R	I
D	R	G	H	E	A	R	T	B	V	C	X	I	N
Z	E	S	F	I	C	O	O	K	I	E	S	P	C
T	S	Y	R	A	S	G	N	J	K	L	R	F	O
R	E	H	A	P	P	Y	B	C	A	R	D	Z	L
P	N	T	Y	J	K	S	M	C	O	E	I	K	N
J	T	C	U	P	I	D	O	L	O	V	E	A	E
I	G	B	X	V	M	O	K	L	S	W	Q	R	P
H	T	G	H	C	A	N	D	Y	K	M	L	D	O
U	H	M	V	X	C	I	P	O	K	R	U	T	E
G	T	C	P	R	E	S	I	D	E	N	T	Y	M
E	A	W	A	S	H	I	N	G	T	O	N	F	B

Name ______________________________

Just for Fun: Make More Words

Directions: Using only the letters from the words *Valentine's Day,* see how many new words you can write. Put a number beside each word you write so you will know how many you thought of.

Name ____________________

Story Starter: My Groundhog

It is Groundhog Day. This year, a groundhog in your yard was chosen to be *the groundhog.* Everyone wants to know if it sees its shadow. People from all the TV networks are at your house. They have asked you to be on television. They want you to tell all about your famous groundhog. What happens next? Write about it.

Name ___________________________

Following Directions: How to Make a Valentine Box

For Valentine's Day, some people make valentine boxes. To make a valentine box, start with a cardboard box. You will also need red and white paper, scissors and glue.

First, cut a hole in the top of the box. The hole is so people will be able to drop valentines in the box.

Next, cover the box with paper. Be sure to glue the paper well. You want your valentine box to look neat.

After the box is covered with paper, you can decorate it with more paper. Cut out hearts and other shapes. Glue them to the box.

When the box is decorated, set it out for everyone to see. It is now ready to hold lots of valentines.

Questions: Literal Comprehension—Recalling Sequence

1. What do you do after you cut a hole in the box?

____

____

____

2. After you cover the box with paper, what do you do?

____

____

____

Name ____________________

Thinking/Writing Page: What Do You Think?

Look at the picture of the pretty valentine. What do you think it says inside the valentine? Write what you think it says.

Name ______________________________

Fantasy: The Giant Valentine

Tim and Mike were at school. They were walking down the hall. Everyone else was in class.

Tim and Mike went around the corner. Then they saw *it!* They saw a *giant* valentine! It was red. It had arms and legs. And it had a face!

"Hi, boys," said the valentine. "I'm here because it's Valentine's Day. Is your class having a party? I like parties."

"Yes," said Tim. "Our class is having a party. Would you like to come?"

"I'd *love* to," said the giant valentine. "Show me the way."

So Tim and Mike took the giant valentine to their party. All their friends were very happy to have a giant valentine there. They played games and they had good things to eat. Soon it was time for the party to be over.

"Well, I have to be going," said the giant valentine. "But I'll be back next year on Valentine's Day."

"See you next year!" said all the boys and girls.

Question: Critical Comprehension—Distinguishing Fantasy from Reality

1. Could the things in this story really happen? Why or why not?

____

____

____

____

READING AWARD

______________________________ **Is Presented**

With This Award For:

____

____

____

Signed ____________________

Date ____________________

MARCH

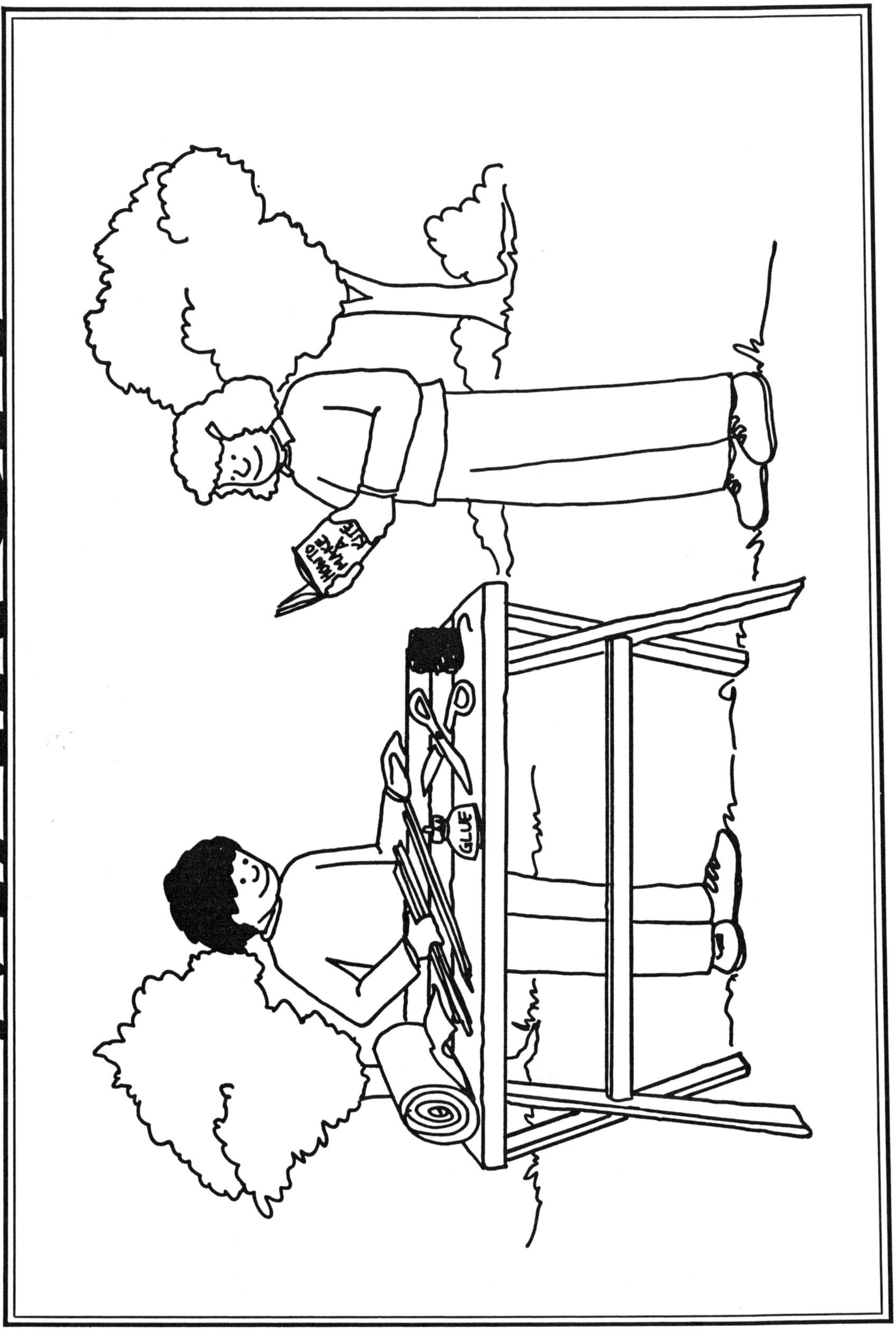

MY FAVORITE FOODS

Name ____________________

Rebus Story: The Windy Day

 Connie and  Leslie were walking to . The  was very near their  house.

 Leslie was carrying her math paper. Just then, a big wind blew the paper out of her hand!

"Help me get my paper!" said  Leslie.  Connie reached for the paper by a  tree. But the wind blew the paper again before she could get it.

Then the wind blew the paper by some  flowers.  Leslie almost got the paper. But the wind blew it again.

 Leslie watched the wind blow her paper by a  doghouse. There was a great big  dog in the  doghouse. "I think I'll just tell my teacher I lost my paper!" said  Leslie.

Questions: Literal Comprehension—Recalling Details

1. Who lost her math paper?

____

2. What happened to the paper?

____

Handwriting Practice

Name ______________________________

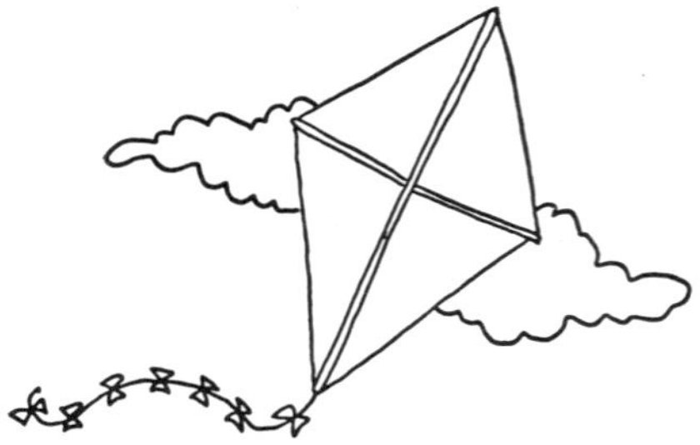

Name ____________________

Nonfiction: March

Spring begins in March. People who live where winters are cold are happy when spring comes. The leaves grow back on the trees. Birds build their nests.

Flowers start coming up in the spring. Sometimes there will be a late snow after the flowers have started to grow. Then there will be little flowers peeking out of the snow!

March is often a windy month. Because it is windy, many people fly kites in March. Sometimes people make their own kites. They like to watch their kites go up, up, up!

March 17 is St. Patrick's Day. Sometimes there are parties on that day. People wear green on St. Patrick's Day. They wear green so other people won't pinch them!

Questions: Creative Comprehension—Responding Emotionally

1. What do you like best about spring?

____

____

____

2. How do you feel about people getting pinched for not wearing green on St. Patrick's Day?

____

____

____

Let's Write a Letter

Name ____________________

Biography: Jim Thorpe

Jim Thorpe was born in Oklahoma on March 28, 1888. He went to school in Kansas. Then he went to the Carlisle Indian School in Pennsylvania.

At Carlisle, Jim played football. He was a very good football player. In the summer, he played baseball. He was a very good baseball player, too.

In 1911 and 1912, Jim Thorpe was on the All-American football teams. Then, in 1912, he went to the Olympics in Sweden. Thorpe won two big events in the Olympics. He got gold medals for winning those events.

Thorpe's medals were taken away from him in 1913. Someone found out he had been paid for playing baseball. People who get paid for playing ball cannot win in the Olympics.

Thorpe died in 1953 when he was sixty-five years old. In 1983, the gold medals he won were given back to his family. Some people say he was one of the greatest athletes of all time.

Questions: Creative Comprehension—Responding Emotionally

1. Would you like to go to the Olympics like Jim Thorpe did? Why or why not?

____

____

____

2. If you won a gold medal in the Olympics, what would you do? How would you feel? On the back of your paper, write about what it would be like to win a gold medal.

Name ____________________

MARCH

Sunday	Monday	Tuesday	Wednesday	Thursday	Friday	Saturday

Name ____________________

Words to Use in Your Writing

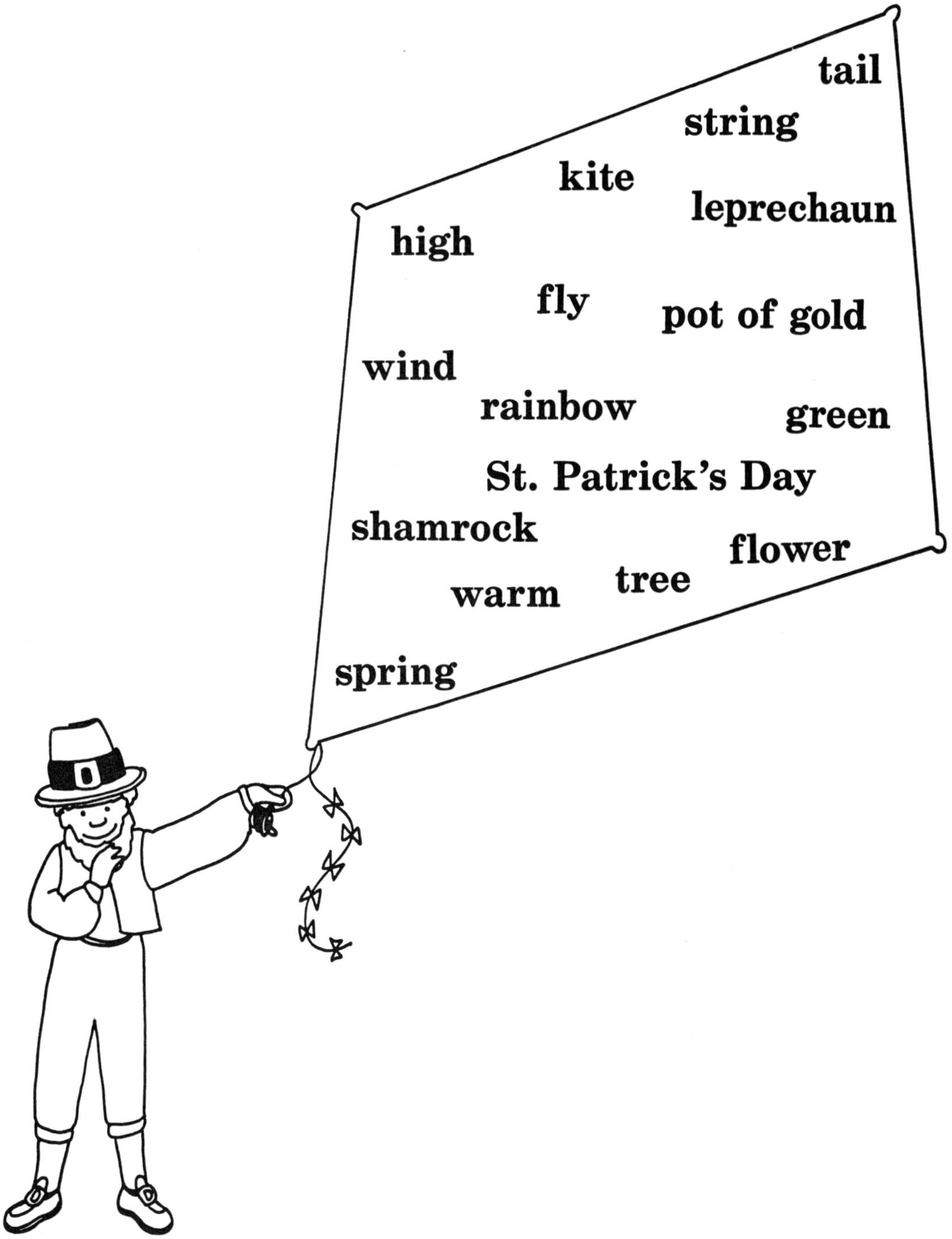

MARCH

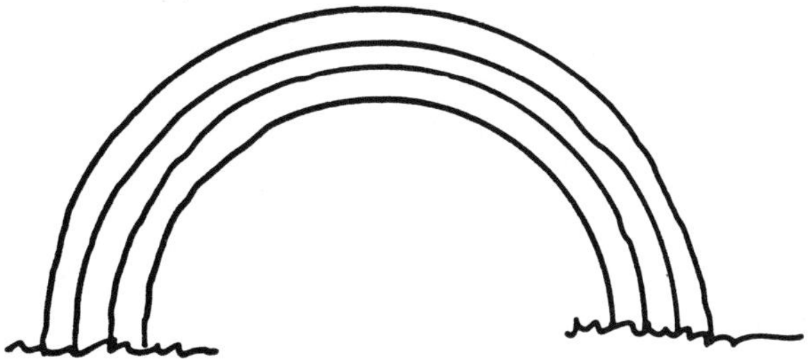

Name ____________________

Book Report

Title: ____________________

Author: ____________________

What the Book Was About:

My Reaction to the Book:

Name ____________________

Fiction:
Making a Kite

Emily and Ryan were making a kite. Emily had gotten a book at the library. The book told all about how to make kites.

First, they glued the wood together. Then they put the rest of the kite together. After that, they made a tail for the kite.

Emily and Ryan liked the kite they made. "This is really a neat kite," said Emily.

"Do you want to fly it?" asked Ryan.

"Yes," said Emily. "Let's fly it."

So Emily started running with the kite. As she ran, the wind blew the kite higher and higher. Emily worked hard to keep the kite flying.

Just then, Ryan looked up. The kite wasn't flying any more. The kite was in a tree.

Questions: Inferential Comprehension—
Drawing Conclusions and Predicting Outcomes

1. How did the kite get in the tree?

____

____

____

2. What will Emily and Ryan do next?

____

____

____

Name ______________________________

Play: Working Together

Characters:	Connie	Mike	Props:	three chairs
	Emily	Ryan		one small stuffed dog
	Leslie	Tim		one small plastic bowl
	Girls	Boys		

(The three chairs are placed in a row. The stuffed dog is under the middle chair.)

Girls: *Everyone is playing in Ryan's yard. Ryan's new puppy, Mickey, is there, too. Suddenly, Mickey runs into the drainpipe under the driveway. He won't come out!*

Ryan: Somebody help me get Mickey out! He won't come out of the drainpipe!

Emily: He's making a lot of noise! Why is he barking so much?

Tim: I think he's scared. Maybe he's too scared to come out.

Connie: I'll call him and see if he'll come to me. Here, Mickey. Here, Mickey.

Mike: Ryan already tried calling him. It didn't work. Mickey won't come out.

Boys: *They called Mickey. But Mickey won't come out. How will they get Mickey out of the drainpipe?*

Leslie: Maybe we could sing to Mickey. Maybe he'll come out if we sing to him.

Ryan: That's a good idea. Mickey likes me to sing to him.

Emily: What should we sing? What song do we all know?

Tim: We can sing "Jingle Bells." We all know "Jingle Bells."

Connie: It's March! Nobody sings "Jimgle Bells" in March!

Mike: Mickey doesn't know it's March. He won't care. Let's sing "Jingle Bells" since we all know it.

(The children sing "Jingle Bells.")

Leslie: Well, that didn't work. Mickey is still in the drainpipe.

Emily: Yes, and he's barking even louder now!

Tim: Maybe he didn't like our singing!

Girls: *They sang to Mickey. But Mickey won't come out. How will they get Mickey out of the drainpipe?*

Ryan: I know. Maybe he's hungry. I'll give him some food.

(Ryan puts the small bowl beside one of the end chairs.)

Leslie: He's not coming out to eat. Maybe he isn't hungry.

Connie: I have an idea! Let's try everything at once! We can call him. We can sing to him. And we can give him food. Maybe that will work.

Mike: That's a good idea. Let's try it. Ryan and Connie can call Mickey. Tim, Emily, and I can sing to Mickey. And Leslie can give food to Mickey.

(Ryan and Connie call Mickey. Tim, Emily, and Mike sing "Jingle Bells." And Leslie holds a bowl near one of the end chairs. When the song is over, Leslie reaches in and picks up the stuffed dog.)

Ryan: Hey, it worked! Mickey came out! By working together, we got Mickey out.

(Ryan takes the stuffed dog from Leslie. He gives the dog a big hug.)

Boys: *By working together, they got Mickey out. Hooray! Hooray! Hooray!*

Name ____________________

My Journal

____

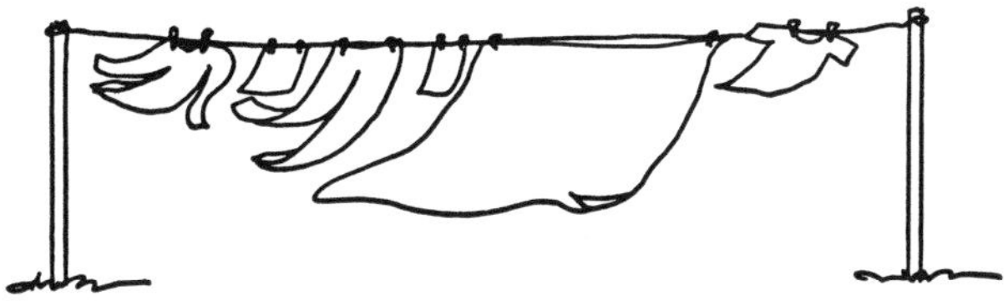

Name ______________________________

My Poem

____

____
____
____
____
____
____
____
____
____
____
____
____
____
____
____
____

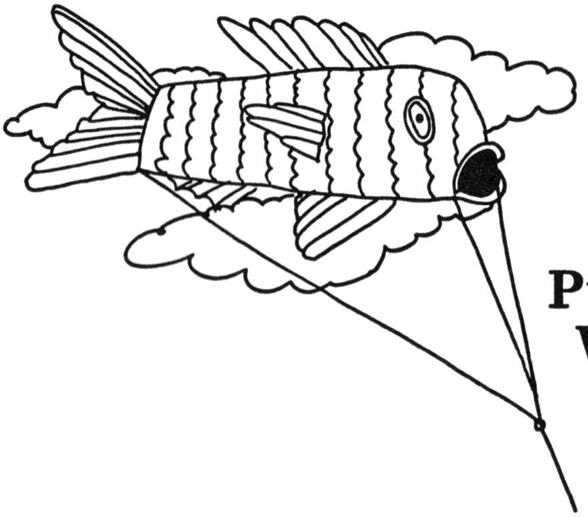

Name ____________________

Puzzle Page: Word Find

Directions: Look for these words and circle them when you find them: flower, fly, gold, green, high, kite, leprechaun, rainbow, shamrock, spring, string, tail, tree, warm, wind.

T	G	S	H	A	M	R	O	C	K	R	F	W	L
M	I	F	D	G	O	L	D	Q	S	A	L	X	I
R	K	F	J	B	V	U	K	L	N	D	O	Z	R
D	I	S	S	T	R	I	N	G	I	D	W	W	A
S	T	X	F	D	J	G	L	H	W	R	E	P	I
S	E	F	A	F	L	Y	G	L	I	M	R	Z	N
Y	H	L	U	I	N	F	J	K	N	W	D	X	B
S	T	R	H	I	G	H	I	J	D	P	G	N	O
T	A	Y	U	N	R	F	G	J	L	W	R	Q	W
R	I	K	E	S	P	R	I	N	G	P	E	H	F
G	L	K	W	A	R	M	M	D	N	I	E	R	T
Y	H	G	L	K	E	S	C	V	G	J	N	L	R
K	L	E	P	R	E	C	H	A	U	N	C	X	E
D	S	Z	L	P	R	T	G	I	K	D	S	N	E

Name ____________________

Just for Fun: Riddles

Directions: Read each riddle. Then answer each riddle by drawing a picture below it.

1. I am soft, and I smell nice. I may be red, blue, yellow, orange, pink, or purple. I grow in the ground. What am I?

2. I have a string and a tail. I can go up in the air on windy days. What am I?

3. I am made up of many colors. You can sometimes see me if the sun is out when it is raining. What am I?

4. I am a little person who wears green clothes. People like to write stories about me. You can see pictures of me on St. Patrick's Day. What am I?

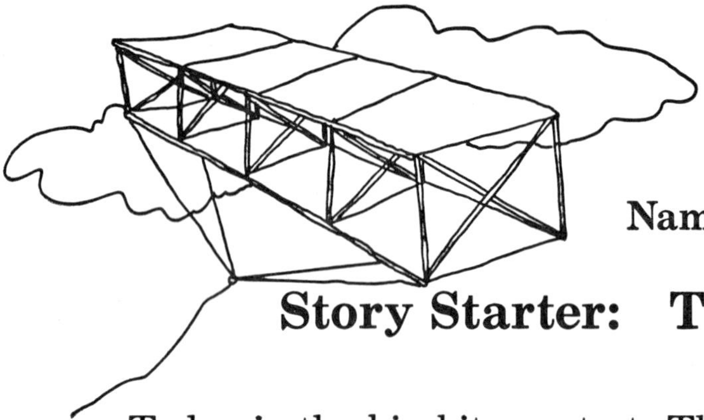

Name ______________________

Story Starter: The Kite Contest

Today is the big kite contest. The person whose kite flies the highest wins the contest. You worked very hard on your kite. You take it to the park and get ready to fly it. What happens next? Write about it.

Name ____________________

Following Directions: How to Make a Pinwheel

You can make a pinwheel to go on the end of your pencil. First, cut out the square below. Next, cut along the dotted lines. Be careful not to cut past the word *stop* on each line.

After you have finished cutting, pick up one corner with a dot on it. Pull the corner to the center. Then do the same thing with the other corners that have dots on them.

When all four corners are in the center, put a thumbtack through the center. Then stick the thumbtack in your pencil eraser. Now you are ready to blow on your pinwheel and watch it go around and around.

Questions: Literal Comprehension—Recalling Sequence

1. What do you do after you cut out the square?

____

____

2. After you pull the corners to the center, what do you do?

____

____

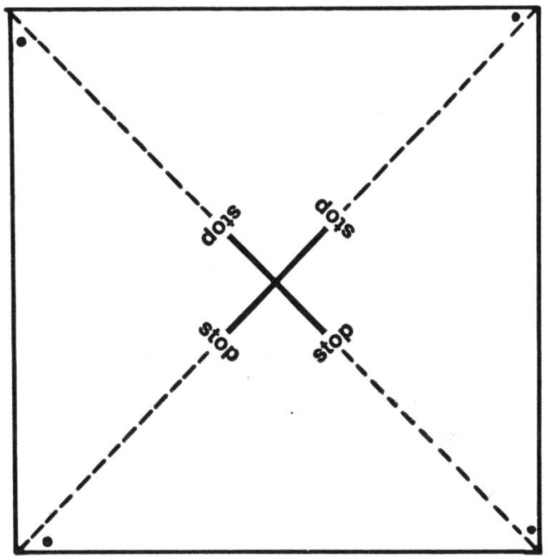

Name ______________________

Thinking/Writing Page: What If?

What if you had wings and could fly? Where would you go? What would you do? Write about what it would be like.

Name ____________________________________

Fantasy: The Little Leprechaun

Mike and Tim were walking in the woods by Mike's house. They had been talking about St. Patrick's Day. Just then they saw a pretty rainbow.

"I heard that if you can catch a leprechaun," said Mike, "that you can get him to tell you where a pot of gold is. It should be at the end of the rainbow."

Just then a little leprechaun ran past Mike and Tim. "After him!" said Tim. "If we can catch him, he can tell us where the gold is."

So Mike and Tim ran after the little leprechaun. The leprechaun ran fast. But Mike and Tim ran faster. At last, they caught the little leprechaun.

"What do you want?" asked the leprechaun.

"We want you to tell us where the gold is," said Mike.

"Why didn't you say so?" said the leprechaun. "I have so much gold that I don't know what to do with it all. I'd be glad to give some of it away. Wait here and I'll bring you some."

So Mike and Tim waited for the little leprechaun to come back with the gold. They waited and waited and waited. Soon it was almost dark. The boys had to go home. They never saw the leprechaun again.

Question: Critical Comprehension—Distinguishing Fantasy from Reality

1. Why do you think this story could not really happen? Write your answer on the back of your paper.

READING AWARD

________________________ Is Presented

With This Award For:

____

____

____

Signed ________________________

Date ________________________

APRIL

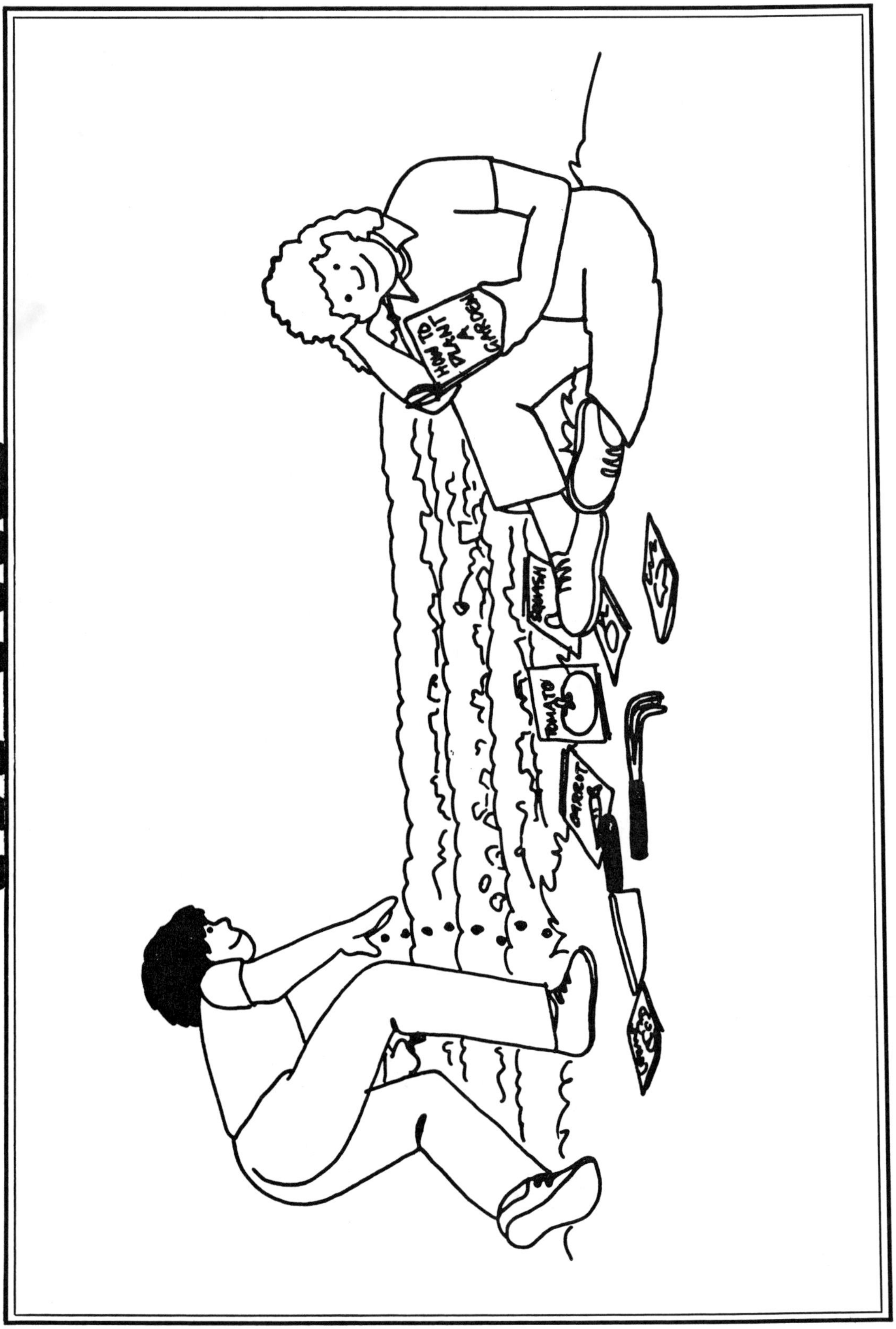

THINGS THAT MAKE ME HAPPY

Name ____________________________

Rebus Story: The Egg Hunt

It was the day of the big egg hunt. 

and 

had been waiting a long time for this day to come.

and 

got out their 

and went to the egg hunt. Many of their friends were there, too.

When the hunt started, 

was the first one to find an egg. It was a pretty green one. She put it in her 

.

Then 

found three eggs. They were yellow, pink, and blue. She put them in her 

.

When the egg hunt was over, both girls had lots of eggs in their 

. They sat down to count all the pretty eggs.

Questions: Literal Comprehension—Recalling Details

1. Which girl found the first egg?

____

2. What did the girls do when the egg hunt was over?

____

Handwriting Practice

Name ____________________

Name ________________________________

Nonfiction: April

April is a time for new life. Baby animals are born. We often see pictures of baby rabbits, chickens, and ducks.

April is usually a rainy month. People say that April showers bring May flowers. Some places may still get some snow in April. But in most places it is too warm to snow.

Easter is usually on a Sunday in April. Easter can be in March. But it is in April more times than it is in March. Some people have Easter egg hunts. They have lots of fun hunting for the pretty eggs.

National Library Week is also in April. Libraries have special events during that week. Librarians help people learn about all the good books that can be found in the library. Library Week is a good time for you to check out a special book!

Questions: Creative Comprehension—Responding Emotionally

1. What do you like best about the month of April?

____

____

____

2. What do you like best about going to the library?

____

____

____

Let's Write a Letter

Name ______________________________

Biography: Wilma Rudolph

Wilma Rudolph was born in 1940 in Tennessee. She was very sick as a child. Being so sick made her crippled. She couldn't walk until she was eight years old. Her family worked and worked with her until she could walk—and run.

Wilma went to high school in Clarksville, Tennessee. In high school she was a star basketball player. She was also a runner. Later, she was a runner in college.

In 1960, Wilma Rudolph went to the Olympics in Italy. She won three gold medals in track-and-field events. Rudolph was the first woman from the United States to win three gold medals for running.

In 1961, Rudolph set the world's record for the women's 100-meter dash. She also won several other awards for running.

After Rudolph quit running, she worked with young girls. She helped start track-and-field teams for them. She wanted the girls to have a chance to run like she had.

Questions: Creative Comprehension—Responding Emotionally

1. Do you think Wilma Rudolph worked so hard at running because she was sick as a child? Why or why not?

____

____

____

2. What do you know how to do that you could teach someone else? On the back of your paper, write about what you could teach other people.

Name ______________________

APRIL

Sunday	Monday	Tuesday	Wednesday	Thursday	Friday	Saturday

Name ____________________

Words to Use in Your Writing

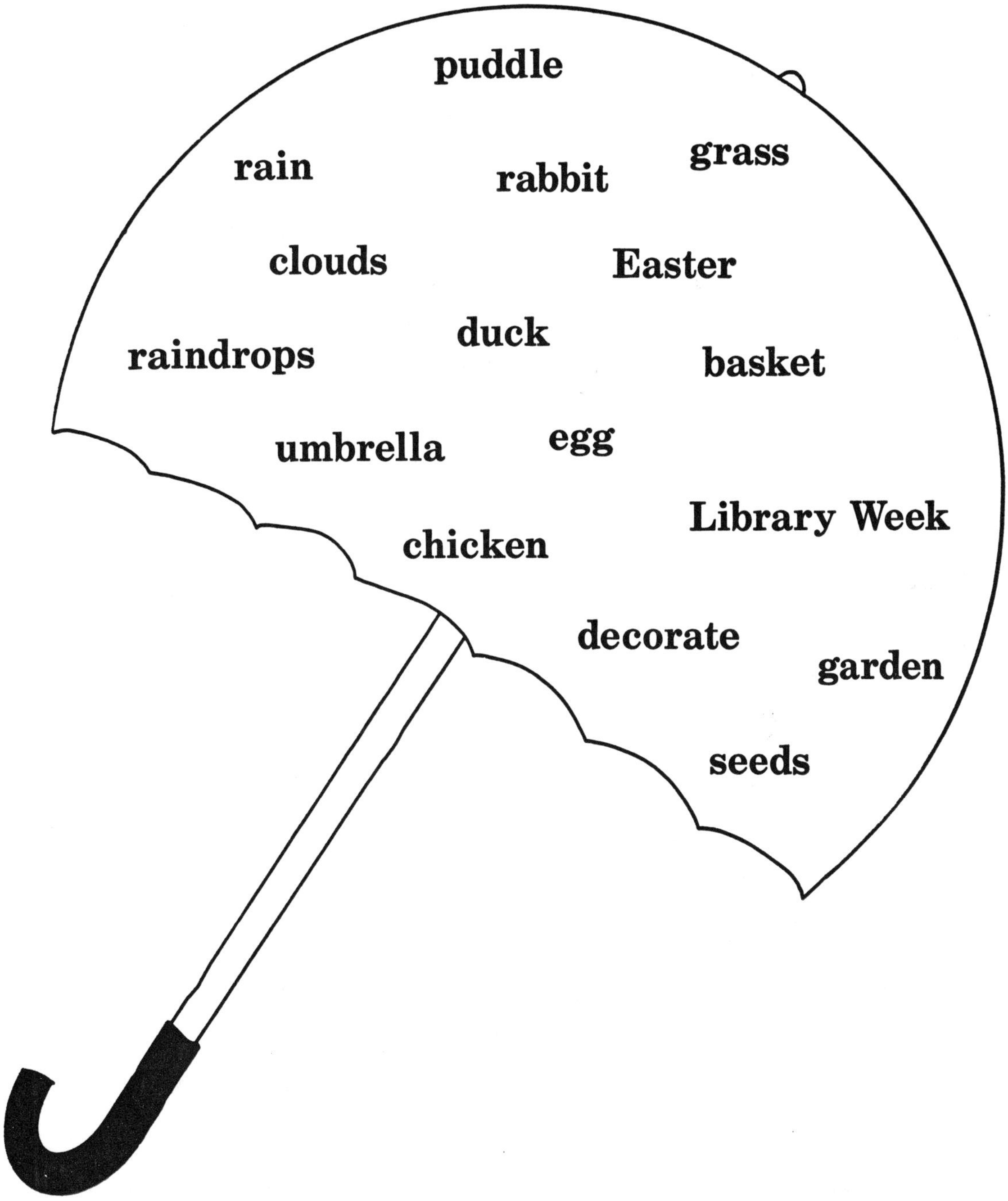

APRIL

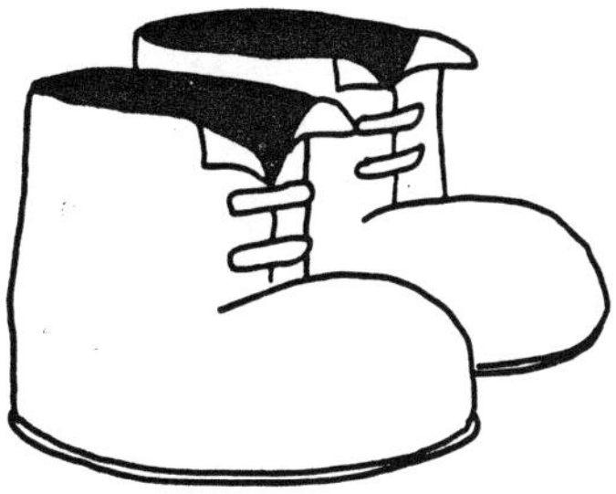

Name ______________________

Book Report

Title: ______________________

Author: ______________________

What the Book Was About:

____

____

____

____

____

____

____

My Reaction to the Book:

____

____

____

____

____

____

Name ____________________

Fiction: Planting a Garden

Ryan and Emily wanted to plant a garden. They got all the things they needed. They got seeds and shovels. They got a book about gardens.

The ground had already been plowed. The dirt was ready for the seeds. So Ryan and Emily opened the seed packages and started putting the seeds in the ground. They planted pretty flowers. They planted many kinds of vegetables.

After the seeds were in the ground, Ryan and Emily covered them with just enough dirt. Then they put everything away and went inside.

In the next few weeks, the garden got just enough rain. It got plenty of sun. Soon the little plants started to come up.

Questions: Inferential Comprehension—
Drawing Conclusions and Predicting Outcomes

1. What made the seeds grow?

____

____

____

2. What will Ryan and Emily do in the garden during the next few weeks?

____

____

____

Name ____________________

Play: The Camp-out

Characters: Ann, Joy, Kim, Girls, Don, Tim, Ty, Boys

Girls: *It is a warm day in April. The children are trying to think of something to do.*

Kim: What can we do? Can anybody think of something we can do?

Don: We could go swimming.

Joy: No, we can't go swimming. The pool isn't open yet.

Tim: We could have a camp-out.

Ann: People have camp-outs at night. My mom won't let me stay outside all night.

Ty: We could have a daytime camp-out!

Kim: That's a great idea! Let's have a daytime camp-out!

Boys: *So the kids are going to have a daytime camp-out. Where will they have their camp-out?*

Joy: We can have the camp-out in our backyard. I'm sure my dad will let us.

Kim: I can bring our tent. We can set it up in Joy's backyard.

Ann: We need to have a fire to cook on. But a fire would burn the grass. How can we have a fire that won't burn the grass?

Ty: I know! We can have a fire in a barbecue grill! I'll bring our grill.

Girls: *So they are going to have a tent. And they are going to have a fire. What else do they need?*

Tim: We'll need something to eat. I can bring hot dogs and buns. We can cook the hot dogs over the fire.

Don: I can bring potato chips and lemonade.

Joy: I'll bring paper plates, paper cups, and napkins. We'll need those things.

Ann: OK. Then I'll bring some cookies. My brother made some last night.

Boys: *So they all go home to get the things they need for their camp-out. While they are gone, it starts to rain. First it rains just a little. Then it rains really hard!*

(Tim calls Ty on the telephone.)

Tim: Ty, what should we do? It's raining too hard to have our camp-out.

Ty: I asked my mom, and she said we can have it in our basement. She'll fix the hot dogs for us in the kitchen. So call everybody and tell them to bring their stuff and come on over! We can still have our camp-out!

Girls and Boys: *It's raining hard. But the children are still going to have their camp-out. Now they can call it a camp-in!*

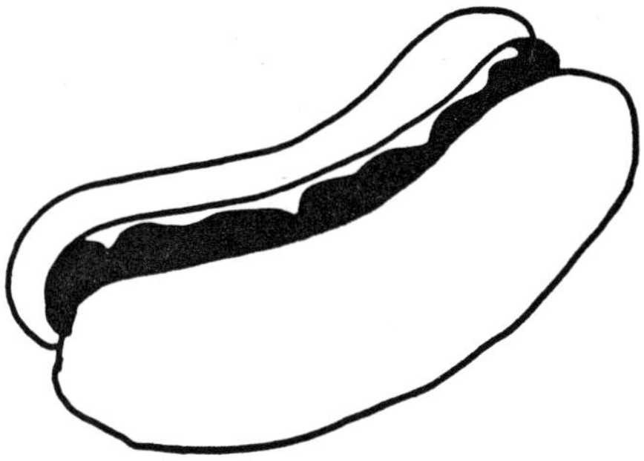

Name

My Journal

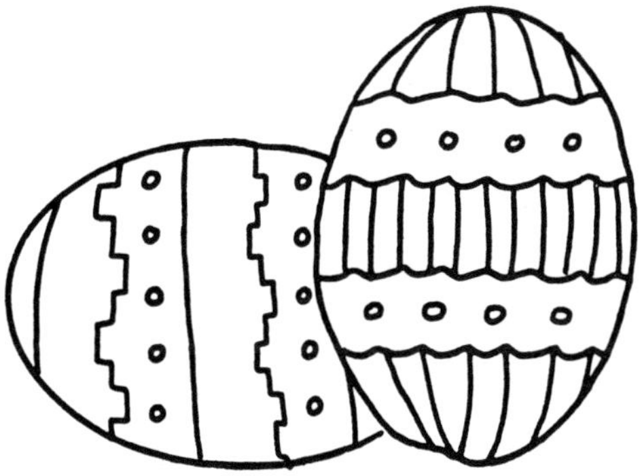

Name ______________________________

My Poem

Name ____________________

Puzzle Page: Word Hunt

Directions: Look for these words and circle them when you find them: basket, chicken, clouds, decorate, duck, Easter, egg, garden, grass, puddle, rabbit, rain, raindrops, seeds, umbrella.

T	X	R	A	I	N	D	R	O	P	S	E	O	W
Q	R	W	P	D	F	I	H	J	O	F	V	X	C
U	W	X	E	A	S	T	E	R	P	J	L	P	L
M	Q	S	F	Z	R	A	B	B	I	T	J	U	O
B	H	Y	J	K	D	S	V	N	E	O	W	D	U
R	P	W	C	H	I	C	K	E	N	D	C	D	D
E	R	W	C	G	K	H	I	N	S	X	C	L	S
L	X	A	W	K	G	A	R	D	E	N	R	E	O
L	F	H	S	E	E	D	S	G	X	I	D	E	Q
A	K	M	V	I	E	W	K	D	J	G	U	E	Z
R	E	T	F	H	B	A	S	K	E	T	C	X	R
O	G	T	H	G	R	A	S	S	L	P	K	W	A
E	G	I	P	G	H	L	J	K	M	C	S	Y	I
R	Y	D	E	C	O	R	A	T	E	L	J	U	N

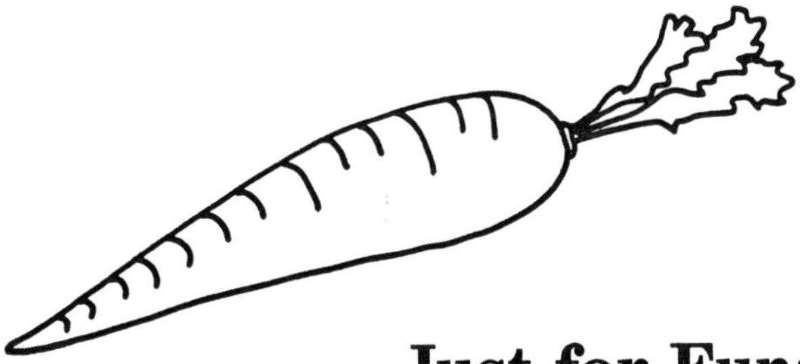

Name ______________________________

Just for Fun: The Rabbit Story

Once there was a rabbit named Roscoe. He had long, floppy ears. He wore a blue straw hat between his ears.

Roscoe liked bright clothes. He wore red pants and a yellow shirt. Roscoe also liked bright shoes. He wore bright green tennis shoes.

Draw a picture of Roscoe.

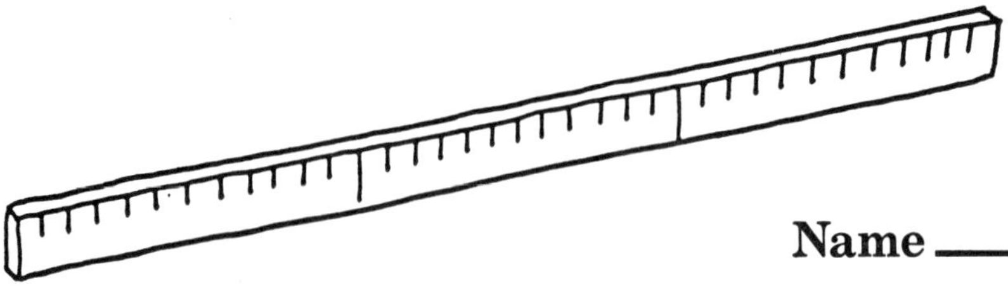

Name ______________________________

Story Starter: Getting Taller

One morning you woke up and said, “I wish I could be taller.” By breakfast, you had grown 3 inches taller. By lunch, you had grown 7 inches taller. By supper, you had grown 1 foot taller. What will you do? Write about it.

Name ____________________

Following Directions: How to Plant Bean Seeds

You don't have to have a garden to plant bean seeds. You can plant bean seeds in a milk carton!

Save a milk carton from lunch. Open up the top all the way. Then wash out the inside and let it dry.

When the carton is dry, cut the top off. You will need only the bottom part.

Next, put dirt or potting soil in your milk carton. Don't fill it too full, or it will spill out!

After the dirt is in the carton, put in three or four bean seeds. Then cover them with dirt.

Now your beans are ready to grow. But you will need to help them. Put them in a sunny place. And sprinkle a little water on the dirt. Later, when the dirt feels dry, sprinkle more water. Soon your bean plants will be peeking out at you.

Questions: Literal Comprehension—Recalling Sequence

1. What do you do after you cut the top off the milk carton?

____

____

____

2. After you cover the seeds with dirt, what do you do?

____

____

____

Name ________________

Thinking/Writing Page: Write What You Think

Write what you think the sad person is sad about. Write what you think the happy person is happy about. Then write what needs to be done to make the sad person happy.

Name ____________________

Fantasy: The Magic Rug

Tim and Mike were at Tim's house. They were sitting on a small rug on the floor. They both were trying to think of something to do.

"I wish we could think of something to do," said Tim. "We've played all my games. Can you think of something fun to do, Mike?"

"No. I can't think of anything to do," said Mike. "I wish this rug was magic. Then it could take us to some fun places."

Just then, the rug they were sitting on started to move. It started to go up in the air. Then it flew right through the door. The door wasn't even open!

"Oh, boy!" said Tim. "Your wish came true. We are really flying. The rug is taking us places!"

"Look down!" said Mike. "There is our school. There is the pool where we go swimming in the summer. And look at the cars. They look so little!"

Tim and Mike flew all around the city. They saw houses, cars, trees, and many other things.

"Oh," said Tim. "It looks like it might rain. We don't want to get wet. I wish we could go home now."

As soon as Tim said *I wish,* the rug turned around. It headed back to Tim's house. It went through the door again. And it landed on the floor.

"Can you think of anything to do now?" asked Tim.

Question: Critical Comprehension—Distinguishing Fantasy from Reality

1. Is this story about something that could really happen? Why or why not? Write your answer on the back of your paper.

READING AWARD

________________________ Is Presented

With This Award For:

____

____

____

Signed ________________________

Date ________________________

MAY

IF I HAD THREE WISHES

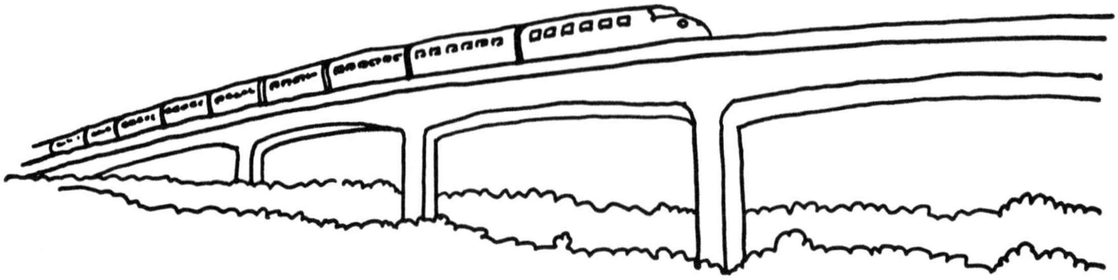

Name ____________________

Rebus Story: Helping Mother

On the day before Mother's Day,  and  got up early. Their mother was going to go shopping all morning.

As soon as their mother left,  said, "Let's do something nice for Mom. Let's help her by doing some of her work for her."

"OK," said . "We'll start by making the . As soon as the  are made, we can wash the ."

"Then we can wash the ," said . "Later, I can clean the  while you fold the ."

The girls worked hard all morning. When their mother got home, she was so happy. "This is the best Mother's Day surprise I've ever had!" she said.

Questions: Literal Comprehension—Recalling Details

1. When did the girls surprise their mother?

____

2. What did they do to surprise her?

____

Handwriting Practice

Name ______________________

Name ________________________________

Nonfiction:
May

May is much warmer than March or April. There are more flowers in May. May is a very pretty month to be outside.

In some places, school gets out in May. In other places, school is not over until June.

Mother's Day is on the second Sunday in May. On that day, people honor their mothers. They give them cards or presents. Some children make pretty things to give to their mothers on Mother's Day.

Memorial Day also comes in May. It is a holiday. The post office and other places are closed. It is the day people honor those who died in wars.

Another special day in May is May Day. It is on the first day of May. A long time ago, boys and girls made little baskets and put flowers in them. They hung the May baskets on people's doors. Then they ran away before the people saw who brought them the flowers!

Questions: Creative Comprehension—Responding Emotionally

1. What do you like best about warm weather?

____

____

2. Think of all the things your mother does for you and your family. Write about the things she does. Use the back of your paper if you need to. (If you do not live with your mother, write about whoever you live with.)

____

Let's Write a Letter

Name ____________________

Biography: Mother Teresa

Mother Teresa was born in 1910 in Yugoslavia. When she was twelve, she knew she wanted to be a nun. She went to India when she was eighteen and became a nun there.

Mother Teresa taught in a high school in India for twenty years. She was also a principal for a few years.

When Mother Teresa was thirty-six, she left teaching and went to help poor people. She lived in the slums. There she helped people who were poor and people who were sick.

In 1979, Mother Teresa was given the Nobel Peace Prize for the work she did to help other people.

In the United States, the second Sunday in May is Mother's Day. On that day, we honor our mothers. Mother's Day is also a good day to think of Mother Teresa. She was like a mother to many, many people.

Questions: Creative Comprehension—Responding Emotionally

1. Does it make you feel good to help other people? Why or why not?

____

____

____

2. Pretend that Mother Teresa is visiting your school. What will you ask her? What will you tell her? On the back of your paper, write about what you would say if you met her.

Name ________________

MAY

Sunday	Monday	Tuesday	Wednesday	Thursday	Friday	Saturday

Name ____________________

Words to Use in Your Writing

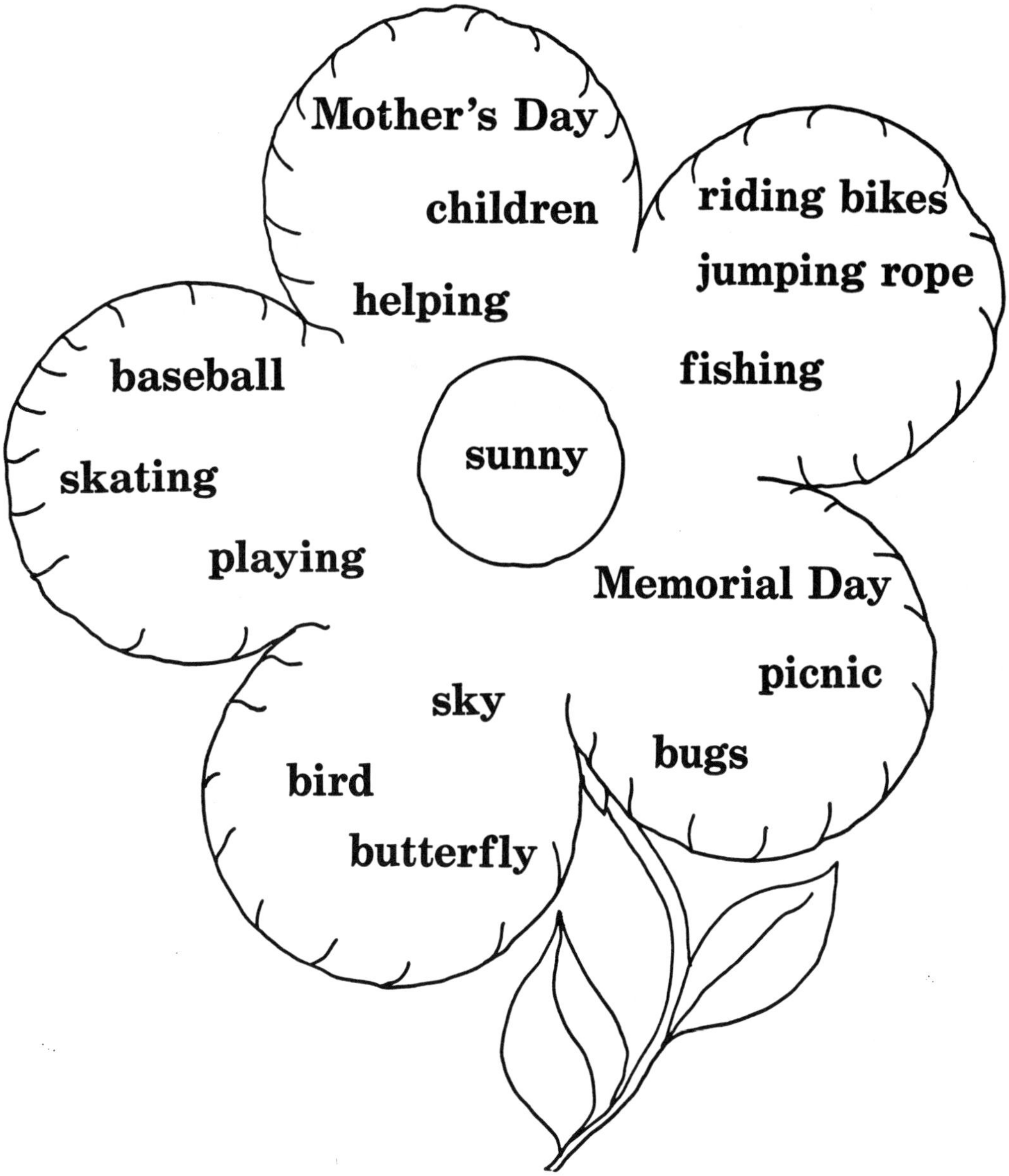

MAY

Name ____________________

Book Report

Title: ____________________

Author: ____________________

What the Book Was About:

My Reaction to the Book:

Name ____________________

Fiction: Reading Books

It was a warm, sunny afternoon. Emily and Ryan were outside reading books.

Emily told Ryan about a book she was reading. Then Ryan told Emily about a book he was reading. They liked to tell each other about books they were reading.

After they read for a while, Emily and Ryan went to play on the swings. They left their books outside.

Soon it was time to go inside. Emily and Ryan went to where they left their books. When they got there, they saw Emily's dog. Emily's dog was chewing up their books!

Questions: Inferential Comprehension—
Drawing Conclusions and Predicting Outcomes

1. How did Emily's dog get the books?

____

____

____

____

2. What do you think Emily and Ryan will do next?

____

____

____

____

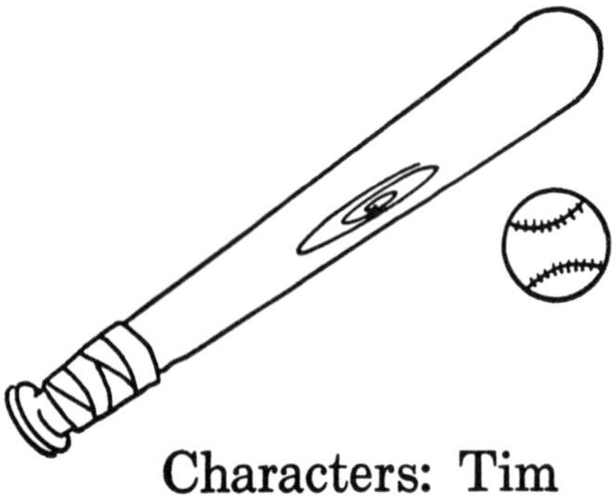

Name ____________________

Play:
Playing Baseball

Characters: Tim, Ty, Mike, Boys, Anita, Ann, Rachel, Girls

Props: three baseball bases made from poster board
one home plate made from poster board
one small baseball bat
one foam rubber ball

(The bases and home plate are set up like a small baseball field. The bat and ball are by home plate.)

Boys: *It is a warm day in May. The children are getting together to play baseball.*

Tim: Hi, everybody! Do you want to play baseball?

Anita: We can't. We don't have enough people!

Girls: *They don't have enough people. How can they play? How can they play?*

Ty: We can still play. I'll tell you how. I'll be the pitcher. (Ty picks up the ball. Then he walks to where the pitcher should stand.)

Anita: Where should I go?

Ty: You can play first base. (Anita walks to first base.)

Tim: Where do you want me to play?

Ty: You can play second base. (Tim walks to second base.)

Ann: Where should I play?

Ty: You can play third base. (Ann walks to third base.)

Mike: What do you want me to play?

Ty: You can be the catcher. (Mike walks to home plate and stands behind it.)

Rachel: All the places are taken. What will I play?

Ty: You will be the first batter. (Rachel walks to home plate. She picks up the bat.)

Anita: I still don't see how we're going to play. We only have one batter. What will we do if Rachel gets a hit and

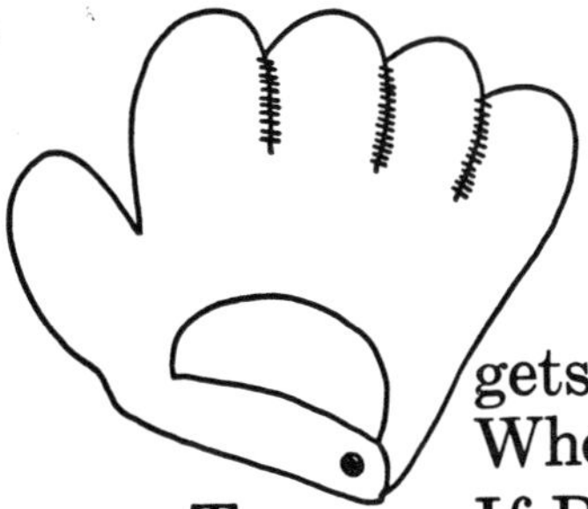

gets on base? What will we do if she makes an out? Who will be the next batter?

Ty: If Rachel gets a hit and gets on first base, she'll trade places with you, Anita. Then you will be the batter. And she'll play first base.

Tim: Oh. I get it. If Rachel gets on second base, she will trade places with me.

Anita: And if Rachel gets on third base, she'll trade places with me.

Mike: So if she gets a home run, will she trade places with me?

Ty: Yes, if Rachel makes a home run, she'll trade places with you, Mike. Then she'll be the catcher.

Rachel: What if I make an out?

Ty: If you make an out, you'll trade places with me. Then you'll be the pitcher. And I'll be the batter.

Boys: *So Ty came up with a way to play. Will it work? Will it work?*

(Rachel holds the bat as if she is ready to hit the ball. Ty gets ready to throw the ball.)

Ty: Here it comes, Rachel. Are you Ready?

(Ty throws the ball. Rachel hits the ball. She makes it to second base.)

Tim: That was good, Rachel. Now I get to be the batter.

(Rachel stands behind second base. Tim goes to home plate and picks up the bat. He holds the bat as if he is ready to hit the ball. Ty gets ready to throw the ball.)

Ty: Here it comes. Are you ready?

(Ty throws the ball. Tim swings and misses the ball.)

Ann: That was strike one, Tim. Try again.

(Ty throws the ball. Tim swings and misses again.)

Mike: Strike two, Tim. Try to hit the next one.

(Ty throws the ball. Tim swings and misses it a third time.)

Rachel: Strike three. You're out. Now you trade places with Ty. You'll be the pitcher. And he'll be the batter.

Tim: Hey, I like this game! Everybody gets to play. Even when I strike out, I get to keep playing. This is fun!

Girls: *They don't have enough people. But they are still getting to play. What fun! What fun!*

Name ________________________________

My Journal

____

Name ______________________________

My Poem

Name ______________________________

Puzzle Page: Word Seek

Directions: Look for these words and circle them when you find them: baseball, bird, bugs, butterfly, children, fishing, helping, jumping, mother, playing, picnic, riding, skating, sky, sunny.

Y	R	G	H	P	K	F	M	O	T	H	E	R	Q
R	Q	B	U	T	T	E	R	F	L	Y	U	I	M
W	C	X	K	J	M	Z	A	Q	H	J	C	D	L
G	B	J	C	H	I	L	D	R	E	N	B	V	P
K	A	M	F	H	E	L	P	I	N	G	T	Y	L
W	S	Q	X	C	L	J	R	T	P	I	V	C	A
R	E	W	S	C	F	I	S	H	I	N	G	P	Y
N	B	K	K	G	H	J	D	S	K	A	R	T	I
Q	A	Y	A	U	B	I	R	D	Z	L	I	T	N
M	L	N	T	Q	W	B	U	G	S	P	D	A	G
G	L	M	I	P	E	V	C	X	Z	T	I	L	J
T	Q	W	N	N	S	K	Y	J	D	T	N	U	E
L	J	D	G	S	U	S	U	N	N	Y	G	O	K
J	U	M	P	I	N	G	X	P	I	C	N	I	C

Name ____________________

Just for Fun: Word Endings

Directions: Copy each word on the line below it. Then add an *ing* to the word. *Remember,* if a word ends in *e,* drop the *e* before adding *ing.* After you have written each new word, draw a picture below it that shows what the word means.

jump	ride	play
1. ______	2. ______	3. ______
skate	fish	help
4. ______	5. ______	6. ______

Name ______________________

Story Starter: The Picnic

Your class is having a picnic. Everyone has brought good food. Before it's time to eat, you are playing games with your friends. You are having a good time. Suddenly, it starts to rain. What happens next? Write about it.

Name ____________________

Following Directions: How to Make a Mother's Day Necklace

You can make your mother a necklace for Mother's Day. All you need is yarn and some straws.

Cut a piece of yarn that is about 1 yard (3 feet) long. Then cut up some plastic straws. Make the straw pieces different sizes.

Next, tie a big knot at one end of the yarn. This is so the straws will not fall off the end.

Now start stringing pieces of straws on the yarn. You can string as many or as few as you like. But leave at least 4 inches of yarn at the end.

When you have enough straw pieces on the yarn, tie the two ends of the yarn together. Now the necklace is ready to give your mother for Mother's Day.

Questions: Literal Comprehension—Recalling Sequence

1. What do you do after you cut a piece of yarn?

____

____

____

2. After you have enough straw pieces on the yarn, what do you do?

____

____

____

Name ________________

Thinking/Writing Page: Let's Pretend

Pretend that someone gave you and your family plane tickets. This summer, you can go anywhere in the world you want to go. Where will you go? Why? What will you do there? Write about it.

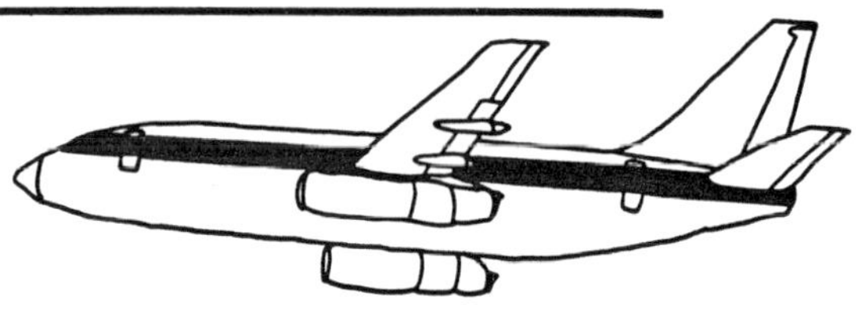

Name ____________________

Fantasy: Making Things Happen

Mike and Tim were at Mike's house. Mike had to clean up his room. His mother said he could not go out to play until his room was clean.

"I hate to clean my room!" said Mike. "I want to go out and play. I don't want to clean this messy room!"

"I saw someone on television," said Tim. "She just moved her nose. She could make things happen by moving her nose."

"It won't work for me," said Mike. "See."

Mike moved his nose. When he did, the bed made itself up. He moved his nose again. Then all his clothes hung themselves in the closet. He moved his nose again. His toys put themselves on the toy shelf.

"I can make things happen!" said Mike. "I moved my nose and my room cleaned itself!"

"That's great!" said Tim. "Are you ready to go out and play now?"

Question: Critical Comprehension—Distinguishing Fantasy from Reality

1. What makes you think this story could not really happen?

____

____

____

____

____

READING AWARD

_______________ Is Presented

With This Award For:

____

____

____

Signed _______________

Date _______________

Name ____________________

Books I've Read This School Year

1. ____________________
2. ____________________
3. ____________________
4. ____________________
5. ____________________
6. ____________________
7. ____________________
8. ____________________
9. ____________________
10. ____________________
11. ____________________
12. ____________________
13. ____________________
14. ____________________
15. ____________________
16. ____________________
17. ____________________
18. ____________________
19. ____________________
20. ____________________
21. ____________________
22. ____________________
23. ____________________
24. ____________________
25. ____________________
26. ____________________
27. ____________________
28. ____________________
29. ____________________
30. ____________________

ANSWER KEY—SEPTEMBER

Page 1-3 Rebus Story

1. Leslie bought pencils and glue.
2. Connie bought pencils, paper, and glue.

Page 1-5 Nonfiction

1. Answers will vary.
2. Answers will vary.

Page 1-7 Biography

1. Answers will vary.
2. Answers will vary.

Page 1-13 Fiction

1. Answers will vary but may include something about either the new principal or the substitute teacher.
2. Answers will vary but will probably say that Emily and Ryan like school because they are in the same class and they know some of the other children in the class.

Page 1-18 Puzzle Page

L	B	G	I	R	L	S	T	B	O	Y	S	W	D
D	R	E	O	D	B	V	W	M	R	C	I	S	A
P	F	X	K	F	R	I	E	N	D	S	Z	J	W
E	R	W	R	I	T	E	Q	S	I	Y	D	S	R
N	H	Z	I	O	V	H	T	Y	I	B	U	L	E
C	B	T	E	A	C	H	E	R	E	O	W	X	A
I	R	J	K	T	H	I	N	K	R	O	F	S	D
L	E	Q	Z	P	U	N	B	Y	D	K	D	X	L
E	S	T	L	E	A	R	N	R	U	G	F	O	B
R	C	X	P	U	T	G	K	D	E	S	K	R	U
I	H	F	C	V	M	O	P	E	F	I	T	Y	S
T	O	U	G	L	U	N	C	H	R	W	Q	V	M
D	O	R	V	I	D	X	M	Y	N	R	U	J	K
E	L	X	C	H	A	L	K	B	O	A	R	D	J

Page 1-19 Just for Fun

The students will cut apart the letters and spell the words listed on the page.

Page 1-21 Following Directions

1. You put one cup of salt in the bowl.
2. You add water a little at a time.

Page 1-23 Fantasy

Answers will vary but should include that dogs cannot talk.

ANSWER KEY—OCTOBER

Page 2-3 Rebus Story

1. They ate popcorn, apples, and candy.
2. Leslie made a jack-o-lantern.

Page 2-5 Nonfiction

1. Answers will vary.
2. Answers will vary.

Page 2-7 Biography

1. Answers will vary.
2. Answers will vary.

Page 2-13 Fiction

1. Answers will vary but may include something about Emily and Ryan picking up the pots and pans.
2. Answers will vary but will probably say that Emily and Ryan are no longer scared because they found out what made the loud noises.

Page 2-18 Puzzle Page

Y	H	A	L	L	O	W	E	E	N	I	P	E	R
F	D	C	V	P	B	M	W	T	R	E	A	T	W
P	G	G	H	O	S	T	E	X	M	K	U	J	W
A	E	Q	W	M	A	S	K	R	T	W	D	X	G
R	C	Q	X	O	P	C	M	V	R	E	S	Z	O
T	O	R	W	I	T	C	H	B	I	O	P	F	B
Y	S	G	F	J	K	I	R	M	C	I	U	S	L
K	T	I	L	E	A	V	E	S	K	I	M	X	I
D	U	R	T	B	A	T	O	D	Q	M	P	V	N
R	M	U	N	E	I	O	R	T	F	W	K	A	S
I	E	I	T	M	C	A	T	X	A	Z	I	Q	W
R	P	G	O	O	D	I	E	S	L	R	N	D	S
Y	X	O	G	K	L	J	R	S	L	C	O	R	I
R	S	K	E	L	E	T	O	N	U	O	P	V	B

Page 2-19 Just for Fun

1. bat
2. mask
3. treats
4. pumpkin
5. spooky
6. ghosts
7. black cat
8. tricks
9. costume
10. goodies
11. goblins
12. party
13. witch
14. skeleton
15. Halloween

Page 2-21 Following Directions

1. You cut out a round place on the top of the pumpkin.
2. You cut out places for the eyes, nose, and mouth.

Page 2-23 Fantasy

1. No. Tim could not really become an astronaut by putting on a costume and closing his eyes, and Mike could not really become a firefighter by putting on a costume and closing his eyes.

ANSWER KEY—NOVEMBER

Page 3-3 Rebus Story

1. Connie is going to check out a book about a horse and a book about flags.
2. Leslie is going to check out a book about a funny rabbit and a book about flowers.

Page 3-5 Nonfiction

1. Answers will vary.
2. Answers will vary.

Page 3-7 Biography

1. Answers will vary.
2. Answers will vary.

Page 3-13 Fiction

1. There is too much food because the children in the class brought too much food.
2. Answers will vary but may say that the class will invite another class to their Thanksgiving feast or that they will share their food with people who do not have enough to eat.

Page 3-18 Puzzle Page

P	R	T	H	A	N	K	S	G	I	V	I	N	G
Y	G	F	K	M	D	R	W	I	O	D	H	E	C
Q	W	D	S	Q	U	A	N	T	O	R	A	O	P
U	Y	G	K	B	X	P	M	R	S	X	T	R	I
P	T	C	O	R	N	T	C	V	P	L	E	U	L
L	J	K	B	R	T	U	R	K	E	Y	P	R	G
Y	Y	R	B	C	V	K	E	M	I	O	U	D	R
M	O	I	W	F	E	A	S	T	R	V	M	P	I
O	M	N	M	R	S	T	A	B	L	E	P	C	M
U	N	D	B	A	Z	P	H	J	M	R	K	I	B
T	B	I	C	O	O	K	J	L	U	K	I	K	P
H	U	A	R	F	A	M	I	L	Y	P	N	E	I
P	T	N	J	L	M	S	D	F	K	R	Y	Q	E
R	S	D	C	V	I	D	I	N	N	E	R	Q	X

Page 3-19 Just for Fun

1. Thanksgiving
2. Pilgrim
3. Squanto
4. table
5. family
6. pie
7. corn
8. Plymouth
9. hat
10. Indian
11. turkey
12. dinner
13. pumpkin
14. cook
15. feast

Page 3-21 Following Directions

1. You put a rubber band around the open end.
2. You make tail feathers.

Page 3-23 Fantasy

1. Answers will vary but should include that people cannot fly through the air or go back to another time.

ANSWER KEY—DECEMBER

Page 4-3 Rebus Story

1. They are going to buy a scarf for their mom and a hat for their dad.
2. They are going to buy books for their grandma and grandpa.

Page 4-5 Nonfiction

1. Answers will vary.
2. Answers will vary.

Page 4-7 Biography

1. Answers will vary.
2. Answers will vary.

Page 4-13 Fiction

1. The smoke alarm went off because Emily and Ryan left their cookies in the oven too long.
2. Answers will vary but may say that Emily and Ryan will throw away the cookies and clean the pan.

Page 4-19 Just for Fun

1.	tree	2.	ornament
3.	candy cane	4.	card
5.	wreath	6.	candle
7.	Santa	8.	sleigh
9.	elf	10.	reindeer
11.	stocking	12.	present

Page 4-21 Following Directions

1. You put the sugar, shortening, and eggs in a bowl.
2. You put the ball of dough on the cookie sheet.

Page 4-23 Fantasy

1. No. People cannot get smaller by eating cheese.

Page 4-18 Puzzle Page

P	W	O	R	N	A	M	E	N	T	S	R	W	Q
R	V	J	I	D	C	R	G	I	F	T	S	X	L
C	M	T	R	E	E	R	F	G	H	H	E	J	S
A	B	G	H	X	L	K	U	E	A	A	D	F	T
N	M	C	J	S	A	N	T	A	T	N	U	I	O
D	I	H	M	J	K	D	S	Y	R	U	O	R	C
L	U	R	C	E	L	V	E	S	T	K	Q	E	K
E	H	I	O	T	G	F	V	I	L	K	O	I	I
W	S	S	C	A	R	D	S	M	I	A	T	N	N
U	T	T	B	M	N	K	E	L	G	H	W	D	G
R	J	M	M	P	A	R	T	Y	H	I	O	E	R
R	Q	A	C	A	N	D	Y	W	T	M	P	E	V
T	G	S	Q	W	B	V	M	N	S	J	I	R	U
W	R	E	A	T	H	R	V	S	L	E	I	G	H

ANSWER KEY—JANUARY

Page 5-3 Rebus Story

1. The girls each put on a coat, a warm hat, a pair of boots, and warm gloves.
2. They built a snowman, a snow woman, and a snow baby—a snow family.

Page 5-5 Nonfiction

1. Answers will vary.
2. Answers will vary.

Page 5-7 Biography

1. Answers will vary.
2. Answers will vary.

Page 5-13 Fiction

1. Answers will vary but will probably say that the snowman in the book will melt.
2. Answers will vary but may say that Emily and Ryan do like to read books because that is what they are doing in the story.

Page 5-18 Puzzle Page

Y	S	N	O	W	F	L	A	K	E	R	P	I	R
E	F	G	B	X	K	W	Q	I	V	X	C	L	J
C	S	F	D	M	I	T	T	E	N	S	M	O	S
O	R	H	T	I	O	P	R	E	D	B	X	V	N
L	G	S	M	B	V	F	R	O	S	T	X	K	O
D	B	N	T	B	I	E	F	H	K	L	S	G	W
D	X	O	R	O	M	K	D	X	S	W	K	P	M
Y	M	W	P	O	V	S	L	E	D	T	A	H	A
S	Q	B	W	T	O	R	F	B	N	M	T	J	N
K	J	A	A	S	M	S	N	O	W	T	E	R	F
I	H	L	J	L	P	O	Y	I	T	V	B	M	R
K	X	L	Q	I	C	E	W	M	E	L	T	S	A
E	C	V	J	K	R	S	D	O	U	A	Y	R	J
W	I	N	T	E	R	C	I	C	I	C	L	E	X

Page 5-19 Just for Fun

1. snowman
2. snowball
3. snowflake
4. snowsuit
5. snowshoe
6. snowfence
7. snowbird
8. snowdrift
9. snowplow
10. snowtire
11. snowmobile
12. snowfall

Page 5-21 Following Directions

1. You cut it out.
2. You tie a piece of yarn through the hole.

Page 5-23 Fantasy

1. People cannot become real football players by putting on football helmets, and they cannot fly through the air.

ANSWER KEY—FEBRUARY

Page 6-3 Rebus Story

1. The party was on February 14, Valentine's Day.
2. They ate cake, cookies, and candy.

Page 6-5 Nonfiction

1. Answers will vary.
2. Answers will vary.

Page 6-7 Biography

1. Answers will vary.
2. Answers will vary.

Page 6-13 Fiction

1. Answers will vary.
2. Answers will vary but may say that the other children will give Ryan some of their valentines.

Page 6-19 Just for Fun

The students will each see how many new words they can make using only the letters in the words *Valentine's Day.*

Page 6-21 Following Directions

1. You cover the box with paper.
2. You cut out shapes and glue them to the box (or you decorate the box with more paper).

Page 6-23 Fantasy

1. No. There is no such thing as a giant talking valentine with arms, legs, and a face.

Page 6-18 Puzzle Page

W	F	V	A	L	E	N	T	I	N	E	R	F	L
G	P	M	H	J	U	F	V	C	X	Q	I	R	I
D	R	G	H	E	A	R	T	B	V	C	X	I	N
Z	E	S	F	I	C	O	O	K	I	E	S	P	C
T	S	Y	R	A	S	G	N	J	K	L	R	F	O
R	E	H	A	P	P	Y	B	C	A	R	D	Z	L
P	N	T	Y	J	K	S	M	C	O	E	I	K	N
J	T	C	U	P	I	D	O	L	O	V	E	A	E
I	G	B	X	V	M	O	K	L	S	W	Q	R	P
H	T	G	H	C	A	N	D	Y	K	M	L	D	O
U	H	M	V	X	C	I	P	O	K	R	U	T	E
G	T	C	P	R	E	S	I	D	E	N	T	Y	M
E	A	W	A	S	H	I	N	G	T	O	N	F	B

ANSWER KEY—MARCH

Page 7-3 Rebus Story

1. Leslie lost her math paper.
2. The paper blew by a tree. Then it blew by some flowers. Then it blew by a big dog in its doghouse.

Page 7-5 Nonfiction

1. Answers will vary.
2. Answers will vary.

Page 7-7 Biography

1. Answers will vary.
2. Answers will vary.

Page 7-13 Fiction

1. The wind blew the kite in a tree.
2. Answers will vary but may say that Emily and Ryan will try to get the kite out of the tree.

Page 7-18 Puzzle Page

T	G	S	H	A	M	R	O	C	K	R	F	W	L
M	I	F	D	G	O	L	D	Q	S	A	L	X	I
R	K	F	J	B	V	U	K	L	N	D	O	Z	R
D	I	S	S	T	R	I	N	G	I	D	W	W	A
S	T	X	F	D	J	G	L	H	W	R	E	P	I
S	E	F	A	F	L	Y	G	L	I	M	R	Z	N
Y	H	L	U	I	N	F	J	K	N	W	D	X	B
S	T	R	H	I	G	H	I	J	D	P	G	N	O
T	A	Y	U	N	R	F	G	J	L	W	R	Q	W
R	I	K	E	S	P	R	I	N	G	P	E	H	F
G	L	K	W	A	R	M	M	D	N	I	E	R	T
Y	H	G	L	K	E	S	C	V	G	J	N	L	R
K	L	E	P	R	E	C	H	A	U	N	C	X	E
D	S	Z	L	P	R	T	G	I	K	D	S	N	E

Page 7-19 Just for Fun

1. a flower
2. a kite
3. a rainbow
4. a leprechaun

Page 7-21 Following Directions

1. You cut along the dotted lines.
2. You put a thumbtack through the center.

Page 7-23 Fantasy

1. Answers will vary but will probably say that the story could not really happen because there is no such thing as a leprechaun.

ANSWER KEY—APRIL

Page 8-3 Rebus Story

1. Connie was the first one to find an egg.
2. After the hunt was over the girls sat down to count their eggs.

Page 8-5 Nonfiction

1. Answers will vary.
2. Answers will vary.

Page 8-7 Biography

1. Answers will vary.
2. Answers will vary.

Page 8-13 Fiction

1. The seeds grew because Ryan and Emily covered them with just enough dirt and because the seeds got just enough rain and plenty of sun.
2. Answers will vary but may say that Ryan and Emily will water the little plants and will pull any weeds that come up near the plants.

Page 8-18 Puzzle Page

T	X	R	A	I	N	D	R	O	P	S	E	O	W
Q	R	W	P	D	F	I	H	J	O	F	V	X	C
U	W	X	E	A	S	T	E	R	P	J	L	P	L
M	Q	S	F	Z	R	A	B	B	I	T	J	U	O
B	H	Y	J	K	D	S	V	N	E	O	W	D	U
R	P	W	C	H	I	C	K	E	N	D	C	D	D
E	R	W	C	G	K	H	I	N	S	X	C	L	S
L	X	A	W	K	G	A	R	D	E	N	R	E	O
L	F	H	S	E	E	D	S	G	X	I	D	E	Q
A	K	M	V	I	E	W	K	D	J	G	U	E	Z
R	E	T	F	H	B	A	S	K	E	T	C	X	R
O	G	T	H	G	R	A	S	S	L	P	K	W	A
E	G	I	P	G	H	L	J	K	M	C	S	Y	I
R	Y	D	E	C	O	R	A	T	E	L	J	U	N

Page 8-19 Just for Fun

The students will each draw a picture of a rabbit with long, floppy ears. The rabbit should have on a blue straw hat, red pants, a yellow shirt, and bright green tennis shoes.

Page 8-21 Following Directions

1. You wash out the inside and let it dry.
2. You put the carton in a sunny place and sprinkle the dirt with water.

Page 8-23 Fantasy

1. No. There is no such thing as a magic rug that people can fly on.

ANSWER KEY—MAY

Page 9-3 Rebus Story

1. The girls surprised their mother on the day before Mother's Day.
2. They surprised her by doing some of her work for her: made the beds, washed the dishes, washed the clothes, cleaned the rug, and folded the clothes.

Page 9-5 Nonfiction

1. Answers will vary.
2. Answers will vary.

Page 9-7 Biography

1. Answers will vary.
2. Answers will vary.

Page 9-13 Fiction

1. Emily's dog got the books because Emily and Ryan left the books outside while they played on the swings.
2. Answers will vary but may say that Emily and Ryan will get the books away from the dog and will try to repair them (or that they will punish the dog!).

Page 9-18 Puzzle Page

Y	R	G	H	P	K	F	M	O	T	H	E	R	Q
R	Q	B	U	T	T	E	R	F	L	Y	U	I	M
W	C	X	K	J	M	Z	A	Q	H	J	C	D	L
G	B	J	C	H	I	L	D	R	E	N	B	V	P
K	A	M	F	H	E	L	P	I	N	G	T	Y	L
W	S	Q	X	C	L	J	R	T	P	I	V	C	A
R	E	W	S	C	F	I	S	H	I	N	G	P	Y
N	B	K	K	G	H	J	D	S	K	A	R	T	I
Q	A	Y	A	U	B	I	R	D	Z	L	I	T	N
M	L	N	T	Q	W	B	U	G	S	P	D	A	G
G	L	M	I	P	E	V	C	X	Z	T	I	L	J
T	Q	W	N	N	S	K	Y	J	D	T	N	U	E
L	J	D	G	S	U	S	U	N	N	Y	G	O	K
J	U	M	P	I	N	G	X	P	I	C	N	I	C

Page 9-19 Just for Fun

1. jumping
2. riding
3. playing
4. skating
5. fishing
6. helping

Page 9-21 Following Directions

1. You cut plastic straws in pieces of different sizes.
2. You tie the two ends of the yarn together.

Page 9-23 Fantasy

1. Answers will vary but will probably say that no one can move their nose and make their room clean itself.